IT´S

MAMA'S

FAULT!™

Mama's Fault?
Truth or Lies?

Post your comments

AND

Join the conversation at:

MamasFAULT.com

IT'S MAMA'S *FAULT!* ™

Poor Decisions
Psychologically Damaging
the Male Child

Lex Drás

GROUP PUBLISHING HOUSE

IT'S MAMA'S FAULT! ™

Poor Decisions
Psychologically Damaging
the Male Child

Group Publishing House, LLC
P. O. Box 723921
Atlanta, Georgia 31139

By Lex Drás

Published by Group Publishing House, LLC
Printed in the United States of America

For a complete schedule regarding bulk purchase discounts and this book in other formats, please click the "Download" Button at:
www.MamasFault.com

ISBN: 978-0-9823070-6-9
LCCN: 2009921398

First Edition. Second Printing

Dedication:

To Nicole,

for motivating me to record on paper

*what **we all know** to be the truth in our minds.*

When things go wrong, we blame Mama.

---Tupac Shakur

ABOUT THE AUTHOR

Lex Drás has demonstrated the ability to overcome and rise above some of life's most horrific challenges (coma, war zones, homelessness, impoverishment, tragic human lose and other misfortunes); unfortunate challenges that could have easily pushed him to the brink of destruction but did not.

Through the extremely loving mentorship (and care) of dozens of VERY wise men and women, the author became an astute student of human behavior, cultural profiles and statistical probabilities, in order to find out how to rebuild his own life. In addition, he attributes these understandings (not just through formal training but VERY REAL life experiences) in part, to: what he has learned living amongst the indigent, extensive psychological military training, living throughout the United States and abroad, travels to remote parts of the world and as a graduate of The Wharton School. Behavioral Observations were/are keen contributors to his survival, especially when confronted with language barriers, *extreme* cultural differences and racial stereotypes. He now has the privilege of sharing his observations with you, from a very personal, uniquely qualified, vantage-point.

AUTHOR'S NOTE

FIRST, let me say that I am extremely appreciative of your deciding to invest some of your money and more importantly your time in exploring the "Poor Decisions" that are rendering devastating consequences to our community and sharing (eventually) your solutions with the world.

SECOND, this book is not about bashing Mothers but a book to enlighten Women; based on the premise ...you must be aware of ___ **before** you can change too ___. With that said, I only ask one thing of you:

READ THE BOOK IN ITS ENTIRETY **BEFORE** making snap judgements about its content. You may be tempted to read segments of the book without doing so from the beginning: DO NOT! If you do, you may very well miss the context, of statements you select, thus assuring your deviating from the overall message. You might as well have missed the boat completely. When you finish reading the book, you may not agree with my assessments but you will certainly understand my reasoning. So, before you get mad, finish reading the book first.

On numerous occasions, I have had the displeasure of tactfully pointing out to reviewers, their ignorance of short-cutting the logical explanations when they arrived at totally emotional responses. Statements such as: This guy hates women; He must have been abused as a child; This guy is looking to use women as scapegoats for all of his miserable failings. In all probability, you don't know me. However, for those women who do know me, know that none of those statements are true. My first response to emotional reviewers is usually in the form of the question, "Well, have you read the book in its entirety?" My already knowing the answer, based upon their response, they would inevitably say, "No, I haven't." Later, they would tell me that after taking a closer look at the subject matter, what they initially saw as insulting or appalling made more sense once devoid their emotional hype.

GUARANTEED! The biggest misunderstandings, during the online forums, will come from those who have not read the book in its entirety but will claim they did in order to keep from looking stupid. Please do not let this be you! If you are going to make comments about what I wrote, which I tremendously encourage and *everyone* (online forum) will look forward to viewing, please let it be in the context of what I wrote, not what you thought I meant and certainly not out of an emotional outburst. If you do, I will "call you out" on it! When referencing text, just research the index to make your point.

Okay! Let's get started and I look forward to meeting you at the end... which will be the beginning?

Lex Drás

p.s. KEEP READING!

DISCLAIMER

This book contains the opinions and ideas of the author. Sold with the understanding and intention of providing informative material on the subjects addressed in the book, it does not contain legal, financial or other professional advice. Individuals requiring such services should consult a competent professional.

The author and publisher make no representations about the suitability of the information contained in this book for any purpose. This material is provided "as is" without warranty of any kind.

Although every effort has been made to ensure the accuracy of the contents of this book, errors and omissions can occur. The publisher assumes no responsibility for any damages arising from the use of this book or alleged to have resulted concerning this book.

This book is not completely comprehensive. Some readers may wish to consult additional books for advice. The "Recommended Reading" section of this book contains a partial list of those additional sources of information.

Changed are the names, dates and identifying characteristics of people in this book.

IT'S MAMA'S *FAULT!*™

Poor Decisions
Psychologically Damaging
the Male Child

TABLE OF CONTENTS

Chapter 2
Selection of Guys   45

Chapter 3
The Five Mistakes   67

Chapter 4
Lies to The Son   79

Table of Contents

Chapter 8

The Wrong Stuff   141

Chapter 9

What the Future Holds   153

PREFACE

Let's fast forward to the end before we begin, in all to say that this book is not finished. You may say, "What!" Yea, it's not finished nor will it ever be because prosperity and change are a never ending process.

This book is the beginning of an *evolving document* and only an introduction to what we already know. If there is something that is missing from these pages, it is because <u>YOU</u> didn't put it there! But hey, don't fret! We are going to try something new. We are going to give you the opportunity to rectify that shortcoming by allowing you to submit your input, give your 2¢ and put your money where your mouth is.

Why are we going to give you that opportunity? We are going to give you that opportunity because this book is only one man's opinion. Granted, there is a huge consensus behind what the author thinks but change is not going to come from **one** man or **one** group or even **one** community. It will come from a collective of minds, people and ideas to turn this terrible, downward trend around. Throughout this book, the author will remind you to state your opinions and do *your* part in an online forum. We at Group Publishing House believe this is the best way to solve problems: Get them out of the dark and into the open, in order to pick them off one-by-one! If the pages that follow apply to you then take them to heart. If they do not, help some one whose life is struggling beneath the weight of such burdens. Using Bill Cosby's words, "Come On, People!" This may be society's burden but it is our problem... THAT'S RIGHT... our problem and it is up to us to fix it!

GPH

INTRODUCTION

This book is going to be difficult for you to read — and maybe even hurtful to you — and you may get angry.

There are ten million exceptions to everything I say. Nonetheless, Everything I Say Is True!

—Dr. Laura Schlessinger

INTRODUCTION

GOOD WOMEN ARE PREVALENT

This book identifies the effects of the African-American single mother's sexual behavior on the male child's psyche and the damage it causes to the race. The book points out how and why women make very poor decisions, leading to promiscuous behavior that produces (in the case of this book) male children, out of wedlock. The continuation of those same poor decisions is destroying the Black Community today! Based on the results they are producing and without any doubt, Black Single Moms, with illegitimate offspring, exhibit a different set of values and beliefs from those women who **decide** not to have illegitimate children.   This does not mean that Single

> *Truth hurts – not the searching after; the running from!*
>   --John Eyberg

Moms, in such circumstances, are all-bad women; in fact, they are some of the nicest women you may ever meet. So, what is the author's issue? Well, it is not a personal issue but a very serious societal problem that is severely effecting the Black Community disproportionately; the problem of the Black Male's plight and its impact on society as a whole and not only in the community where he may live. A tremendous percentage of EVERY problem in the Black Community today **STARTS** with the birth of a child bore out of such circumstances.

There are plenty of high quality, very productive, intelligent women in our midst. The author knows there are because he has had the honor and privilege of working with, living amongst and loving a wide cross section of Black Women throughout this great country of ours. Cross sections consisting of women of all sizes, political leanings, educational levels, economic standings, social classes and religions apart from the Protestant faiths. Understanding and identifying quality is easy when, like the author, you continuously observe the template of what encompasses the exceptional woman. The actions of what women *should* do are prevalent in the Black Community. However, it is up to that Community as a whole, to **install** that inclination into the next generation TODAY to prevent the demise of the African-American Race TOMORROW.

THE **ULTIMATE** RESPONSIBILITY

While in the process of compiling data for another book, the author was constantly comforted with "The Question" of who is *ultimately* responsible for teaching the "The Answer" to a child from day one. Since the basis of the "The Answer..." book builds on the concept of installing Foundational Fundamental Principles from day one, it begs to reason that the quality of the teacher(s) is the primary factor in the environment where they are taught. Ideally, it takes a community to raise and teach a child but we all know that is a copout when it comes to responsibility! You may then say it is the responsibility of the extended and immediate family and if pressed further, the parents. The author strongly believes that a community, family or parents cannot teach what they do not know! Yes, they all play a part in the raising of a child but you can narrow the list down even further. The father plays a part in creating a child but ultimately, it takes a mother to bring it into the world. Without the mother, the female component of the species, a child cannot be born. If a child is not born then there is no need to teach to what is not there.

This book is the PREQUEL to "The Answer…" book in that it just **identifies** the problem. "The Answer…" book gives solutions on how to prevent the next generation from repeating the cycle.

> *You shall know the truth and the truth will make you mad!*
> --The Neal Bortz Nationally Syndicated Radio Show

"It's Mama's Fault!" identifies and introduces only one painful truth (the promiscuous behavior of women who carelessly become single mothers), which must be brought to the forefront and addressed in order to decimate it. Pretending it is not there is killing our community.

IT'S JUST AN OBSERVATION

This is not an academic dissertation but a conversational piece. The author did not write this book attempting to be the preeminent authority on illegitimate Black Males in our society but only to bring to the forefront this discussion **by the masses**. Let's be clear! The author is not a psychologist nor psychiatrist and does not proclaim to be one! This is not a sterile, clinical dissection of the Black Male's Behaviors but of only personal observations, which almost any *intelligent* person can relate too. If you want an in-depth, psychoanalysis, of the inner mental workings, of a Black Single Mother with an illegitimate male child then the author suggests you purchase one of those 300 plus page books by a Ph.D. or M.D.! Yes, they will have very well researched and detailed books but the average person on the street will not even attempt to read them let alone implement **ANY** of their strategies! Change will come from the masses not from a few, very well credential, academics at the top; impressive but not *effective.* This book will provide an easy read and a forum, for the masses, where anybody can chime in on the discussion. All the author asks is that you just look at the long-term actions of a man and compare it with the profile of his mother. It does not take a Ph.D. for that! We cannot reduce (nor ever eliminate) the negative effects of Black Male Behavior in society until we focus in on **the cause, from its beginning**. The author believes that the compounding negative decisions of the woman are the *initial* cause.

While watching an old movie, "Road House," starring Patrick Swayze, his character was giving an orientation to his newly acquired staff. One of the comments, from one of the guys, in response to what Patrick's character said was, "So, are you calling my mother a whore?" Patrick's character responded by saying, "Well, is she?" By the behavior exhibited by the guy, in an earlier scene, who asked the question, what his mother is was probably accurate! The point here is that the child will have a very strong tendency to repeat those same behaviors (mentally, physically, socially, etc.) growing-up in that environment. Like father, like son; like mother, like daughter. If mom is a hoe, what do you think her child will be?

INTENTIONS MEAN LITTLE

Good Intentions & Indecision have caused more pain and failure in this world than what the author calls F.E.E.D.: **F**ailed **E**xpectations leading to **E**motional **D**isappointment.

Let's start with the first part of the first sentence, Good Intentions. Nearly everyone has Good Intentions with the birth of a child but VERY FEW have any realistic idea of what to expect when it comes to raising that child in impoverished conditions. Evident by the shear fact of the birth itself, these women were not taught (thoroughly) by previous generations of their families of what could have been easily avoided.

Every problem, every story, every solution has a beginning. We must **start** there to identify it, explain it and take the painful steps to solving it. If only the IDEA of even considering having a child, under reprehensible circumstances in our society, is made to believe unthinkable, deplorable and extremely shameful, the negative tide will reverse. This attitude disseminated into a culture over the course of a generation will have the same effect as a steady antibiotic treatment over the course of weeks to kill an infection. Our problem is that our culture does not see it as a problem so there are not any *effective* treatments implemented to stop (illegitimate births) what is slowly killing us as a race. The painful truth is that no one wants to acknowledge the cause of our Race's decline, which by the author's formula, you cannot take steps to tremendously diminish the problem if you do not want to *accurately* identify it. This book will explain why this decline happens, why it continues and what MUST transpire to reverse our current path towards destruction.

CONNECTIONS

Loneliness. There is not a person alive who has not felt this emotion at some point in their life! What does it mean to resolve it? For most, it means to make some kind of connection. Unfortunately, that connection has

Introduction

a sexual connotation and an overwhelmingly majority of the time it is the wrong type needed. Sex is the most powerful of all emotions in its ability to get us to act. In addition, it is the most destructive in that it can cloud sound judgement leading to very poor, irrevocable decisions. Like the power of atomic energy: It can power almost all of society's energy needs or single-handedly eliminate life on earth, as we know it. These two forces are that powerful. Although sex may be the most powerful of physical interactions, it is not the deepest emotionally. In fact, it is quite shallow. Sex is an emotion, emotions are of the heart and the heart is like a child/subordinate/Indian. Logic and intellect are that of the mind and the mind is like an adult/commander/Chief.

Deeper is mutual respect and admiration. When people seek connections, this is what they really want but all too often do not have the ability to identify it let alone articulate it. Again, sex is a shallow connection and mutual respect and admiration is a deep and long lasting connection. To prove that point, think of it like this. A child as young as ten (these days), engages in sexual acts and intercourse. Most would agree that those actions would constitute a connection, a **physical connection/relations**. However, how many children, that age, can understand the meaning of mutual respect and admiration, a true (healthy) connection at the deepest level? Many adults still do not have a clue about it, let alone a child.

Now, let us explore a **mental relationship**. Once again, The Deep v. Shallow; The Mind v. Heart; The Mental v. the Physical; The Adult v. Child; The Commander v. the Subordinate; The High Road v. Gutter Trail. Both levels are required to produce the whole so this is not to discard the bottom and pretend there is only the top. This is to say that there is a hierarchy. "Connections," for long-term, lasting actions start from the top (leadership), to ignite the bottom (workforce) that will enhance the whole.

The author is not blaming anyone for anything. The author is just holding adults (supposed leaders) accountable for the decisions they make. Some of the decisions we make have grave consequences and as adults, we are ultimately responsible. When was the last time someone told you, "if you don't do _____ you will die?" Let me answer that for you: NEVER! There are those that may say that they were victims of circumstances and my response to that statement is the question, "Who raised, or didn't raise, you?" Whom ever that was, the author suggest you ask them why you are so f#@*~-up! In over 80% of the cases, it was their Mama.

Until society, or specifically the Black Community, brand getting pregnant and having a baby out of wedlock so painful, embarrassing and shameful we will continue to have droves of Black Women, and girls, moving forward with those decisions. The majority, to save face, will say its okay and that there is nothing wrong.   Until powerful mentors stand-up to the inevitable onslaught of criticism sure to come, from those who have already made their choices, we cannot turn the tide. This is likened to when the author was in the military, he could remember three distinct times when "the rules" changed and caused the "old guard" to go into an uproar! However, either they changed with the times or they got out the way (discharged from the Service). We are currently watching the destruction of our people because the "old guard" will not get out the way (in the form of "saving face"), so not to appear hypocritical or just downright stupid.

A WOMAN'S
MINDSET

The truth does not change according to our ability to stomach it.

–Flannery O'Connor

Chapter 1

A WOMAN'S MINDSET

DOMINANT THOUGHTS

Have you ever heard a woman ask, "why do I attract *all* the crazy men into my life" and she was sincere? The answer to that question is simple! If she hangs-out in environments where there are a plethora of losers then that is what she will get. While in that environment, her inner feelings WILL become her outward expression. She needs to hangout with a better quality of crowd so that when her inner feelings do become her outward expression, at least the target has a high probability of being worth-a-damn.

If her inner feelings (subconsciously) are about f#@*\!$, then her outward expression **WILL** reflect those thoughts, whether she would consciously like them to or not.   She MUST be cognizant of the language she uses: Sweetie, love, sugar, baby, etc.; The tonality of her voice: Seductive, cute giggles, etc. and;   Most importantly, her body language: Her proximity from the guy, hugging/embracing upon meeting or leaving, a kiss on the cheek, a stare into the eyes, her hand touching… anywhere. If she is in the presence of someone whose interest she wants to attract (much later and not her initial meeting) then maybe, but absolutely not in a business or business like setting.

Astute men can sense the flicker of a woman's Dominant Thoughts when they meet them.   When women combine it with their language, tonality and body contact, they have just lit a blaze that they may not be able to put out;   advances, and possibly reputations, they may not want.

We inevitably attract into our lives the people and circumstances that harmonize with our Dominant Thoughts. If we want to attract different people and different circumstances, we must change our thinking (and the places we go). Our thoughts are a form of electromagnetic energy, like a magnet, attracts those people and those circumstances that harmonize (same wavelength, path, disposition, background, etc.) with them. If you do not believe in emotional (feelings) control, your ability, to mask your dominant thoughts, is severely compromised. As long as you radiate this dominant feeling (f#@*\!$), you will attract **CRAP** instead of **SUBSTANCE**.

Anytime you are in an intimate setting (designed to relax, bring on euphoric pleasure) where there is music, low lighting, erotic dancing, possibly alcohol; if it's at night, in places like a bar, club or even a private party, you will become susceptible to YOUR Dominant Thought(s).

You can put any label on the affair you want, i.e. networking event, fundraiser, business meeting, etc., but it doesn't matter. Let's be real, if those other elements are present (intimate setting) then your focus ain't on earnest characteristics, its on f#@*\!$.

ANXIOUS?

Anxiety – **Living in fear of** someone finding out the truth of what *really* is going on in your life instead of the fake façade you want the world to see: Better known as upholding an IMAGE (a problem a lot of performers / entertainers [or wanna-be] experience; Fake).

Embarrassment – Someone **actually finding out** the truth as opposed to the phony crap you wanted everyone to believe.

There are a lot of intensely sexual, sensual women in our midst; physically and psychologically expressing a longing sexual desire, depicted in the sultry auras they project! It is reflective in the way they speak, the poetry they recite, the music they sing and in the photos

> *The truth is on the march and nothing will stop it.*
> --Emile Zola

they take. They can't stop it! They wear it on their sleeve, it has gotten them into trouble in the past and will probably do the same in the future. These types of women are in conflict with themselves: Who they are, in conflict with, the image they want to portray to their sons and to polite society.

They find themselves fully wanting to express their sexuality but that expression is constantly being thwarted by their not wanting their sons to *really* know who they are. They secretly engage in activities they are ashamed to admit to anyone (damn sure not to their sons) and with men they will not introduce to their sons because they ain't worth sh**, all to get "what Mama needs." They are in conflict! They lie awake at night, or sleep very restlessly, all due to their hoping no one of important influence finds out what they *really* are; believing that WHEN that façade eventually falls that no one will find them truly loveable (which is probably right except for the crap that will settle for someone with their profile). Wanting to be *truly* loved, the very thing they want the most: from their sons, their family and that very elusive piece… a DECENT man. They ask themselves constantly, "Do I give it all to become this "Sexual Diva" or do I just forget about it all and live an average family life??" Let the author help them narrow it down, the "average family life thing" ain't in the cards!

If a woman is at peace with how she is living (behaviors), then that will be evident by how well she sleeps at night, which means her behaviors are congruent with who/what she is (her core); Women fitting the above profiles are not... they ain't sleeping to well. What they are trying to portray to their sons (the pristine mom façade) and who they *really* are internally is incongruent, that means they are being fake and they deserve to feel like sh**. The author is certain that is just how they fell every morning. They want to f#@*, f#@*, f#@*, every night, wake-up in their own bed and f#@* some more in the morning! But Nooooo, they don't want the sons to see their Mama for what she *really* is; with all those different men coming out of her bedroom every week! Hey, the author has an idea! Let's put in a "cut out" to make it *seem* like the woman is stable with a *boyfriend* when in actuality the woman is f#@*\!$ & sucking some other men on the side! That way, their sons won't think poorly of them. Yea, right! Most sons will need to be damn near retarded to fall for that one but based upon the actions these women produce, they would have to think that their sons are just that!

It is almost impossible to maintain that façade long-term; trying to put forth an image to their sons that ain't who they *really* are. That pressure takes a devastating toll on their psyche and body, which only leads to anxiety attacks, sickness, worry, queasiness leading to diarrhea, sleeplessness, depression and just plain unfulfilled, leaving a huge void; there is nothing she can do to fill that void (*more* men, drugs, TV, food, alcohol, etc.) except for being true to themselves... and their sons! Women must be real and truthful with themselves first, even if it embarrasses their sons (which it will). They need to acknowledge what they are and let the chips fall where they may!!

Let's just say for-the-sake-of-argument the author thinks a woman is a [blank]. Why would the author come to that conclusion? What has caused the author to think that "If it walks like a [blank] and talks like a [blank] (behaviors the author sees and knows about, not what women **try** to hide from their sons) then it must be a [blank]." If that is what they are then that is their business! If this is not what they are then **THEY seriously need to check their actions that give off that perception**.

DRUG OF CHOICE

One June afternoon in 2007, the author was listening to the Michael Baisden Radio Show about "Single Men that Cheat." That lead to a conversation with a woman telling him of a guy with whom she had sexual relations. She said he dated other women in addition to her (he at least admitted it, which [at least] gave her the option of if it was right for her; unlike the examples of men on the radio program). She went on to say that it was shortly after the passing of a family member and that she was in a lot of pain. Being non-exclusive was acceptable to her because she really didn't give-a-f#@* at the time and the only thing she wanted out of it was some sex since it took her mind off the pain for awhile. This story is not an isolated incident amongst women who use sex to stop the pain, during their down moments. The choices females make; some pop pills, some drink, some eat to oblivion and some shop until they drop, while others *get* f#@*?%.

AN ELEMENT OF TRUTH

On how many occasions have you heard a woman say, "Don't judge me!" As human beings, we all pass judgement. It is VERY reasonable to judge a person by the actions they take AND by the associations they make: birds-of-a-feather, flock together. If a woman's behaviors are that of a [blank] and the people they associate with demonstrate the qualities of [blank] then it is not a far stretch to believe they are a [blank]. Unless a woman possess the compartmentalization psyche of a CIA agent, undercover cop or any of the other psychologically trained, covert operatives, they do not have the skill set to hide it... especially from a trained eye.

Frankly, we all evaluate circumstances through the eye of *our* camera, of our upbringing, education, adult experiences and based on the *quality* of people we associate with the most. Fortunately, most intelligent people do not just stop with the stereotypes or first impressions. They continue to evaluate information to make sure it is valid. They will give multiple opportunities to the target subject to confirm or reject their initial assumptions. More times than not, woman do not need to worry about what intelligent people's opinions are of them **IF** their core is genuine and above board. If, however, what they initially detected is real and a woman is acting fake, look out! That woman may just have a problem on her hands!

What other people's opinions are about us really does not matter, until, their CONTRARY thoughts impede upon the actions we want to take **OR** we sincerely want the approval and respect of those we care about (spouse, children, family, close personal friends, professional colleagues, etc.). It is at this time that we want to be on the same page with their values & beliefs and pay attention to their opinions.

You will never stop people from judging you or having an opinion about how you conduct your affairs. It will **always** exist whether, for example, it is of a multi-billionaire with access to everything or of a welfare mom, with multiple kids, having different fathers, living in the projects. Someone is always going to have an opinion: "that rich a**-hole stole all that money he has from poor people" or "that welfare b*tch ain't worth sh**.". However, the difference is in how one

> *Anger at lies lasts forever. Anger at truth can't last.*
> --Greg Evans Luann

party views **NO element of the truth** in a negative statement and the other views **SOME element of the truth** in a negative statement.

When someone passes judgement and there is **NO element of the truth** in a negative statement, the receiving party can very easily ignore the statement because it is not relevant or; make the judging parties look extremely ignorant, stupid and sometimes worthless. When someone passes judgement and there is **SOME element of the truth** in a negative statement, it is ALWAYS offensive to the receiving party. Why? Because now they are embarrassed and know that at some level **the epithet has some relevance** to it. Found out, they try to "save face" by giving every reason in the world for why it was not their fault or that it is not true.

Is there **SOME element of the truth** in the author calling women, fitting "the profile" a particular term? You, as well as the author, know there is.

SELECTION OF GUYS

The truth that makes men free is, for the most part, the truth which men prefer not to hear.

–HERBERT AGAR

Chapter 2

SELECTION OF GUYS

THE VALUE OF BLACK MEN

If you want the answer to why Black Women say *most* Black Men ain't worth sh**, just look at how those men were raised: Were they born into a normal family nuclear structure of the FATHER MARRIED TO THE MOTHER **OR** a Single Mom raising a bastard child. Guaranteed, hands-down, there is a difference.

The first place a boy learns about *real* love is in how the father treats his mother. WHAT HE SEES. If this is f#@*?%-up or heaven forbid, absent, it will have an indelible negative effect on how that boy sees, and tries to initiate, ANY intimate relationship in the future. The chaos theory states that a flaw at the beginning, and not repaired, only gets worse as it moves through the continuum. If you do not stop the problem before it starts (not being born or placed in a quality home shortly after birth) then you will have a problem that you cannot repair later;   the problems that plague a tremendous majority of the African-American Males in society today.

PLENTY OF MALES TO MARRY

NOW the woman wants to get married, after the fact. Okay, if marriage is her objective then that should not be a problem. However, if her objective is to marry a man of substance and quality then a woman with a son will run into some challenges.   What kind of male would marry a woman with a son, not to mention one with multiple kids with different fathers? Answer: A dumb-ass-[blank]. Great News! There are plenty of [blank]s that were raised in that type of environment (as stated in the previous paragraph), that do not think there is anything wrong with it and are right-up the ally of the typical Black Single Mom. There will be no conflict of values & beliefs as to how to raise a bastard child, since both of them will be resident experts on how the Black Male Child can follow their example and thus repeat the cycle for the next generation.

Here are the numbers: 80% of Black Households are run by a single parent and in over 98% of those households, it is the female. As of what percentage of the children were born out of wedlock, the author is not certain but can guarantee that it is an overwhelming majority. With these numbers, a Black Single Mom, with a bastard child, should not have any problem finding a [blank] that will put up with her situation.

Do these last few statements sound ridiculous? Well, if they do then why isn't this *common* practice declining?

THE QUALITY POOL IS SHALLOW

Keep in mind, you will have deviations in the data just like any other statistical inference. So, take this with a grain-of-salt; THERE IS NO SUCH THING AS ABSOLUTES, only probabilities.

There are approximately 39 million Blacks in America, we comprise about 13% of the population. Unlike most races, our Female to Male percentages are not near the 50/50 mark because of the alarming rate at which our Black Males are killing themselves. Instead, the percentages are closer to 60/40 in favor of the Females. This means that there are approximately 15.6 million Black Males in this country and 1/3 of them are under 16, which leaves just under 10.5 million Black Males over the age of 16, in America. The numbers below do not include the percentages that are over 65, gay or physically handicapped. Although not calculated here, the number of Black Males who want to marry a woman, are still capable of having sexual intercourse and are willing to raise children is probably closer to a total of 7 million Black Males. When doing the factoring for the Females, this equates to approximately 10 million viable Black Females vying over only about 2 million *VIABLE* Black Males who are worth-a-damn! On average, this equates to five Black Females for every Black Male: Advantage… The *VIABLE* Black Male! If you factor in women of other races, the Black Woman really has a strong competition issue when it comes down to what the "successful" Black Male is willing to tolerate. The ratios can reach as high as 10 to 1, in his favor, depending on what part of the country he lives.

THE STATISTICAL BREAKDOWN

Asking the Black Woman, what type of guy do you want? Do you want a cool thug [blank] (code for: stupid) or the type of quality emanating from the Cream-of-the-Crop at the top of the socio-economic scale? Black Men raised by a Black Single Mom, out of wedlock, run the gambit from the bottom to the top. However, statistically speaking, you have over 95% of them emanating from the bottom (in, just out of, or headed to prison) of the socio-economic scale than those doing something to contribute to society (neurosurgeon, corporate executives, entrepreneurs), at the top! Here is the categorical breakdown of the Black Male population.

☹ The low end consists of two categories: The first category, is of those who are in prison and those who have served time but are now released (approximately 55% [5.7 million] of the Black Male population).

The second category is comprised of males engaging in activities that will land them in prison (approximately 15% [1.57 million] of the Black Male population).

😐 There is a middle group and it consists of two categories. The first category is comprised of just regular guys that do not have a degree from college, work a 9 – 5, go to church on Sundays, etc. Most are not aspiring to become anything special and are just living day to day (approximately 20% [2.1 million] of the Black Male population).

The second category is made up of guys who have some college, trade school training, military and or and Associates Degree (approximately 5% [just over 500 thousand] of the Black Male population).

☺ The top end of the group consists of two categories. The first category is of College educated men with Bachelors Degrees and those with graduate degrees and beyond (approximately 3% [315 thousand] and 1% [just over 100 thousand], respectively, of the Black Male population).

The second category is an over-all category; comprised of C.E.O's, Professionals or Entertainers. These guys are considered affluent (earning over 150k per year) and/or wealthy (net worth of over 1.6 million). They comprise approximately .08% (just over 80 thousand) of the Black Male population.

SCRAPPING THE BOTTOM

There are four types of guys, who will marry a woman with a son. Is every type of guy listed below a bad person? NO, of course not, but for any man who settles for this type of situation, leads you to question his reasoning why.

☹ **MR. DAMAGED HIMSELF** - The first type of guy we already noted. He is a bastard child himself and if he has siblings, they ain't sharing the same daddy. He does not see a problem with it because it is his life. In fact, he may see this family structure as normal! The problem with this category is that most have NEVER LEARNED how to be a man, FROM A STRONG MAN, in the household. How can this man teach a child what being a man is all about, if his only points of reference come from the losers his mother went through while he was growing-up?

☹ **THE ASSHOLE** - The second type of guy could be like the first guy but is of a worst breed. This guy has a bastard son somewhere else and is NOT RAISING HIM IN THE HOUSEHOLD WHERE HE LIVES! The author has the greatest issue with this type of guy because raising a child is not about the money spent on the situation but **HIS** PRESENCE & TIME spent with the child that makes the difference. The child is really f#@*?% because this is not the type of guy you want influencing your son even if he is around.

☹ **STRAIGHT LOSER** - The third type of guy give men a bad name: No education, no job and no future; probably just got out of prison, is an alcoholic, a drug abuser, etc. Ain't worth-a-damn... for nothing important. The woman with low self-esteem is just happy to have something of the male persuasion where she lives. She will take almost anything that pays her half attention, short of a physical abuser and sometimes the Black Single Mom ain't smart enough to even see that!

The Loser knows that a woman with a son, or kids, is all that he can get. He knows that a woman without children, well-educated, high self-esteem and doing well in the world is only going to deal with an equal or better partner. She will need to be really, really desperate and her self-esteem sunk really low before a high caliber Black Woman will settle for this sh** or any of the other types at *the Bottom*.

☹ **THE UNDESIRABLE** - The fourth type of guy is not necessarily a bad person just at the bottom of the list, of all the potential prospects sought by a high caliber Black Woman.   He may be diseased, has bad internal health, physically handicapped in some way or to old to have children. These guys are willing to deal with a woman with children for one of two reasons. One, since they have no children, or may not be able to have children, they may still want to contribute to the welfare of a child or; Two, a woman with children is all they can get.

THE SOCIAL SCENE

Women, this is how guys think about Social Settings. Regardless of the type of guy you meet, just know that it is going on in their head in some way, shape or form. When in school, the author's Fraternity Brothers would always joke about the quality of the girl by the school she attended or the Sorority she was a member. Every city is different, of course, but there will always be a hierarchy of schools, based on what will be her station in life after graduating college. In Atlanta: A hair dresser: Atlanta Technical College (A typical

Selection of Guys

Community College where if you can fog a mirror then you can get in!); A doctor: Spelman (Prestigious 4 year Institution with very high academic requirements for admission). Etc., etc.

Using Historically Black Colleges & Universities (HBCU's) as examples, the saying in Atlanta goes:

> *A truth that's told with bad intent beats all the lies you can invent.*
> --William Blake

You get your d*** sucked by a slut from Atlanta Technical College; you get your booty-calls from females at Morris Brown; you spend quality time with a young lady from Clark Atlanta (ΔΣΘ-Delta Sigma Theta) and; **you want** to marry a woman from Spelman (AKA-Alpha Kappa Alpha). Using the HBCU's analogy, the author applied them to the following types of Social Settings and where guys "Shop" (for one-nighters, girlfriends, a wife).

The Night Club: (Open to the Public) "Hit-It & Quit-It." No matter what a female is thinking, guys are up in the club, or a bar, to get some a**… tonight; that's what these places are for! If f#@*\!$ is out of the question, so are they; Girlfriend material is a joke. Women stupid enough to think, or expect, otherwise are the epitome of the low quality you do not want!

Now, with that in mind: Why would any self-respecting woman go to ANY type of Club, Night Spot or Bar, with any consistent frequency (more than three times a month), when this is basic common knowledge for any guy with substance?

The women who frequent Clubs, Nightspots and Bars fit in one of the 6 categories:

1. Unmarried Females under the age of 25; It's just what kids do.

2. Just Straight Ghetto hoes (especially those over 30); No Class (Opposite of the description in the sub-heading, "Mark of Quality").

3. Never married but has a kid and if two or more, they are by different men.

4. They are usually two or more of the following: non-college graduates (4 year school), drink, smoke, are obese and out-of-shape and are habitual users of some type of drug to get through the day (illegal or prescription).

5. Divorced, separated or broke-up with a boyfriend: in pain and looking for attention of any sort.

6. Some combo of the first 5.

Everything you want in a future spouse! Yea, right! Does this sound bad? It is but that is how guys, with any substance, think about women who frequent such places.

.................*ATLANTA TECHNICAL COLLEGE*

Night Time "Networking" Event: (Open to the Public; *semi*-professional crowd) Still, "Hit-It & Quit-It." This is just "The Club" for the older crowd. Depending on who is sponsoring them, this type of event is in different locations, every week, throughout a city's metro. The same profile that applies to a female who frequents other nightspots applies here except they are just a little older and possibly with a higher income. Whatever pops off is-what-it-is and like the club, it's no big deal because there will be another "Networking" Event somewhere else next week.

.... *MORRIS BROWN*

Professional Seminars: (Restricted Access; only for registered participants) Permanent Friend. Definitely has something, or could have something, on the ball. Sex is possible but not the goal, so not to hinder what could be very beneficial on a number of fronts. You want this lady on your team, regardless of whether anything happens or not.

....*CLARK ATLANTA*

Invitation Only: (Private Functions) Dating / Marrying Quality, even if she is a b*tch. Invitations to these types of functions are usually from friends or close colleagues. More times, than not, we *usually* socialize with people who are similar to ourselves on some level. Screening naturally takes place to weed out the undesirables from the setting, which you cannot do when an event or club is open to the public. You do not invite people you have a low opinion of to such functions. Logic dictates that if you like your friends then your friends will like your friends. In this case, innocent by association.

When we introduce our friends to our friends, we try to be a bit more discrete not to link our friends up with losers.

If we (guys) find them sexually attractive, we ain't gonna mess-up what could possibly be a serious long-term relationship with sex (that's what Atl Tech's and Morris Brown's are for), or at least not initially. With some of the longest lasting relationships the author knows of, there was no initial sexual pursuit of the other when they first met. In fact, they found common ground in **meaningful settings**, on **purposeful matters** FIRST, before the shallower trivialities were ever put into play.

....*SPELMAN*

THE MARK OF QUALITY

Every guy wants their "Spelman" to be a freak in the privacy of the bedroom and not look like a total whore by their outward appearances and demeanor in the street; A female's Grooming, Body Adornment, Clothing and Attitude all reflect that consciousness.

GROOMING – Conservative hairstyle or head adornment; light (if any) make-up; short neutral nails; a consistently suitable appearance for the occasion.

BODY ADORNMENT – Very tasteful and reserved jewelry (if any), visible piercings limited to the ear lobes, zero tattoos or in very, very discrete personal places.

CLOTHING – Well fitting but not tight, very little skin exposed and if so, it is appropriate; classic styles trump brand names, where you must take the clothes off to identify the designer.

ATTITUDE – Refined disposition, polished presentation, well mannered, articulate, poised, courteous.

As a saying goes: the less you have on the inside, the more you attempt to make-up for those deficiencies by an exaggerated outside: appearance, attitude, material possessions. These are extremely good indicators about upbringing, education, occupation and future objectives without even saying one word to find out more.

Selection of Guys

What is this all to say? It's about how a guy sees, interprets and judges quality. He will place heavy emphasis on how he defines a quality woman based on comparisons to his mother (good or bad), his upbringing, what college he graduated from and his chosen occupation. **IF** this is the type of guy you want (YOUR PURSUIT NOT HIS) and **IF** you want Quality and Substance then **YOU** must appeal to **HIS** definition of Quality and Substance not yours. How does **HE** define Quality and Substance? How does it relate to where you met (a "Morris Brown," "Clark Atlanta," "Spelman" or heaven forbid, a "Atlanta Technical"[straight trash])?

Every guy who is in "the game" (not married) has some version of this setup: If he is in the right circles, he may have a few "Spelman's" to choose from of which he can be proud to call his girlfriend (given certain circumstances on both their parts [school schedules, demanding jobs, different cities, cash flow situation, etc.]). If not, he is sure to have a few "Clark Atlanta's" he respects and with whom he will spend quality time.

When it comes to sexual contact, a smart, *viable* brother is not willing to endanger his quality, possibly long-term, relationships. However, let's not be naive, he is not going to go without either. For this, he calls up "Morris Brown's" for booty-calls and if all else fails, he can always pick up an "Atl Tech" at the club. The bottom line is that if not from the top end of the spectrum (Spelman's), he will go to the bottom (Atl Tech) to "get it the way he likes it" until he is ready to get married. Women, this "game" is a double standard, we (guys) know, but hate on society not the *viable* brother.

WHERE GUYS SHOP

In real estate, there is a term called, "A" Buyers. These are the buyers that can purchase anything they want, within their price range, without needing any special favors, financing or terms, to close a traditional mortgage transaction. The "A" Buyer is VERY METICULOUS and they have every cause to be. They do not need to settle for anything and they are looking to get everything they demand. The "A" Buyer is going to "Shop" in the best neighborhoods, select the best parcels of land and choose the best floor plans. If the house does not have *everything* they want, they will just walk away and go elsewhere.

There are a few guys who are classified as "A" Buyers. Of course, women are not houses and you cannot get *everything* you want but you damn sure can be very selective (as to their state of mind, body, income, social graces and morals). Again, the "A" Buyers are going to "Shop" in selective social circles to find pleasing personalities, what they deem as physically attractive, educational qualifications, etc. Chances are that if a guy is well educated, physically fit, looks halfway decent, earning a substantial income and not gay, he has several, "Spelman," options at his disposal regardless of his personality.

Disagree about it being Mama's Fault?

Tell *your* story

AND

Join the conversation

at:

MamasFAULT.com

The Five Mistakes

You never find yourself
until you face the truth.

–Pearl Bailey

Chapter 3

THE FIVE MISTAKES

SQUANDERED OPPORTUNITIES

How does the strongest force in America get to a point of a continuous downward cycle? Easy, that "force" CHOOSES not to exercise what is in its total control. That "force" **ONLY** has to control **ONE** particular **SITUATION**: Selective Reproduction.

The Black Woman has five opportunities, between nine months but usually much longer, to change for the better the direction of the Black Community, as it relates to the birth of the next generation of African-Americans. She can set the wheels in motion to systematically eradicate poverty, escalate the enrollment of our youth in the finest universities across the country and be the basis of building wealth lasting for generations. However, because of f#@*?%-up decision making, over and over and over again, they destroy that chance EVERYDAY! The only thing she has to say is… **NO**. THAT IS IT! Why is this so hard? Hmmm, let's see.

As with everything, what is learned or not, starts in the home on some level. That level can be mental, physical, financial, social and/or moral & ethical values. Values, reflected in acceptable behavior in society as a whole, are the **ultimate** responsibilities of the **parents** to install; not the *grand*parents, aunts, uncles, schools or the churches. When the **parents** do not, there is a clear delineation between what *Mama* has, or has not, done and the f#@*-up. This is evident

> *I want to tell the truth, and the truth often hurts.*
> --Bill Cosby

with the five avoidable mistakes that a Black Woman has the COMPLETE power to control but does not. The lives of all human beings are designed to be one of two things: They can either be EXAMPLES of what to become or WARNINGS of what not to do. Give whatever excuse you like: Black Women who CHOOSE to continue after the "SECOND *AVOIDABLE* MISTAKE" (below) are not what you call EXAMPLES of what to become.

RECTIFIABLE BAD DECISIONS... ALMOST

1. FIRST *AVOIDABLE* MISTAKE. She hooks up with a loser. Oh well, this happens and dating a loser by itself is not all bad. We all must learn, through experience, what not to do. Girls, just like boys, need the proper guidance and examples to follow in the household, so it probably was not her fault. It was the Mama's Fault for not providing a quality example (**MARRIED** to her father or some other quality guy) from which to learn. The first man a woman *should* love is her father. This figure will serve (whether she is consciously aware of it or not) as the template of what she sees as quality and will gravitate towards. When this figure is absent or not actively involved in the woman's life, guess what

fills the void? A clue: 95% of the time, quality ain't it.

2. SECOND *AVOIDABLE* MISTAKE. She decides to have sex with the loser. Okay, having sex is not bad. The author is not naive enough to believe that we all should abstain until married because that is a lot of bull-sh**! However, the basis upon which sex occurs is of issue, not only to the author but also to a multitude of people. It's almost certain that it is not under the guise of truly caring and understanding the authentic qualities of the person. You may say, "What?" Yea, how the hell can you know what that is if you never learned it at home by watching your parents? The author is sure the sex was under the pretenses of: the girl is horny and/or not wanting to loose the attention of the guy. Attention that she NOW is getting because it was not coming from home. Again, it is the Mama's Fault for not having a quality man around, to teach his daughter what having sex *should* mean and the various consequences to crossing that line, from a **man's prospective**.

The Five Mistakes

3. THIRD *AVOIDABLE* MISTAKE. **SHE decides** to get pregnant by the loser. Sure it takes two to make this happen but it takes one, the female, to realize the consequences of **HER** mistake and its impact on the rest of **HER** life. Oh, the author is sorry, what was he thinking?! This is mute if not taught in the home! This idea falls on death ears when unwedded pregnancy is common place in the female's environment (see Reference Groups in Chapter 8) and not thoroughly ingrained by the parent of what not to do because they have done the same thing! This, of course, is not always the situation but in a devastatingly number of cases it is. Chances are such that Mama did not say to her daughter while growing-up, "I was careless and stupid and you were a fuckin' mistake (pun very much intended) so do not let the same thing happen to you." You know why that mother will not say that to her daughter? She will not say it because that would make Mama look like *she is* careless and REAL stupid not to

---

There are only two mistakes one can make along the road to truth; not going all the way, and not starting.
    --Buddha

---

mention, a slut! In her efforts to save face, rather than stand strong and tell the truth, the downward cycle continues because of pride. Evident by the fact that she is UNMARRIED & PREGNANT, the "It's **your** future that is impacted the most" concept, being taught in the household BY EXAMPLE, was probably far fetched. It is a no-brainer with most conservative families: It is not smart, to get pregnant by a guy, you are not married to, dah!! Again, family examples, family values, what is taught or not, in the household makes all the difference in the world! Married THEN children! Not, "Oh I'm pregnant, let's get married," or "…after the child is born I'll get married to some sucker," trifling ghetto sh**. Or worst of all, "f#@*-it, I'll just have the kid and I don't need no man anyway!"

A tremendously, terribly misconstrued concept of one thinking that just because they give birth to a child does not necessarily make them fit to be a parent! PARENTS LEAD BY EXAMPLE, out front, not by running their mouths with hypocritical rhetoric trying to direct from behind. Black Women who subscribe to the aforementioned **lack** of thinking do not deserve to be parents. This concept applies to everything, not just having illegitimate kids; If you do not know [blank] and have not experienced [blank] then how can you teach it?

4. FOURTH *AVOIDABLE* MISTAKE. She decides to carry the fetus to term. There's a whole lot that can be said about this and most of it ain't positive. Okay, it may be against her morals (or religion) to abort a fetus. Gime-a-f#@*in' break! She already violated half-a-dozen morals before she got to this point, what-the-f#@* is one more! Here we go again, it always comes back to the quality of ones upbringing and the "cast of characters" in her life.

Conservative family's viewpoint: You finish college, you get a job earning a substantial income to support a family, you get married **THEN** you start a **FAMILY** (mommy *married* to daddy, who parent child [what a concept!]).

Black Liberal's viewpoint: F#@*-it! I'll just have a bastard son, I don't need no man to raise *my* son;

besides, my brothers, father(s), uncles and men at the church will be around to help; everybody in my neighborhood does it (this should tell you about the quality of that neighborhood); I'll just figure it all out as I go along from other "high quality" individuals with bastard sons! Does anyone see a problem with this line of thinking (or lack thereof)?

5. FIFTH *AVOIDABLE* MISTAKE. The Black Woman **decides** to keep the child instead of putting it up for adoption, with a family that can raise it properly.

It is at this time everything is out the fuckin' window. Let the downward cycle begin! Now ya got Mama with this son, trying to lead a normal life. An epiphany: she f#@*?% that up when **she decided** to have a bastard child.

DAMAGED GOODS

In wholesale/retail, there is a term called Damaged Goods. It simply means that for whatever reason you are not able to sell the items at the usual full price, you must make concessions and sell them at a DISCOUNT, if to sell them at all. As human beings go for marrying purposes, Single Moms with children are labeled: Damaged Goods. Not **if** she is but it is only a question to what degree; some more than others. Just like any other damaged merchandise, the greater the damage the lower the price, if able to sell at all.

If a woman is fat, she can loose weight; If she is butt ugly, there is makeup and wigs but; If she is stupid, well... there ain't no help! When she has a son, that is irrevocable and you cannot change those circumstances unless it dies!

OVERCOMPENSATING FOR SHORTCOMINGS

One of a mother's greatest fears is of her son having a change-of-heart, towards her, while growing-up; a release from a build-up of anger and resentment for her not providing him with a "normal" family environment to include a father in the home. Every year he gets older, he is going to wonder why he does not have a father around and he is going to formulate opinions about her (subconsciously) as to why. The author is sure mothers of pre-teen boys have seen remnants of this already and it will get worse. If her son is ever fortunate enough to break into the Ivy League and all the prestige, wealth and access it can bring him, he will see a very different world then the one from which he came. The author knows Black Single Moms secretly hope their sons stay "Black" so that they will not see how any of the "normal" families look and operate first hand. As long as he hates White people, or even Black Wealth, they hope to delay this "release" until he is at least out their house by 18.

In that vein, Black Single Moms are over compensating for that paternal presence not being available and that is a VERY big mistake. Those very actions produce weak-ass Black Males. Their attempts to *shield* him from hard work and unpleasant responsibilities to avoid "busting his lip" are the very reasons why so many Black Men ain't worth sh**! Mama-Boys, depending on someone else to do the work because they never learned how (from a man) to do it themselves, during their childhood, in order to survive in a society outside the Black Community.

LIES TO THE SON

Telling the truth... is not solely a matter of moral character; it is also a matter of correct appreciation of real situations and of serious reflection upon them.

–DIETRICH BONHOEFFER

Chapter 4

LIES TO THE SON

CAUGHT AGAIN?

Here is a scenario that I am certain every Black Single Mom, who is sexual active, has contemplated. As one of the author's mentors stated, "It's not what happens to you, it's how you evaluate, interpret and respond to what happens to you that will make all the difference in your life. As this pertains to your (Mama's) activities, how do you respond? Do you respond with *white* lies or the trifling truth?

Here's a situation:

Your son has been spending a lot of time engaging in non-productive activities around the house (watching TV, playing video games, etc.), especially during the non-school months, weeks or days. It progresses to the point where he wakes-up and immediately cuts on the TV, to start his day! You reach the point where you need to force your son, off the couch and to go outside to do something!

Why is your son so reluctant to go outside to socialize with the other kids in the neighborhood? There can be a number of reasons but there are most likely only a few: Either he is anti-social or he does not want be teased or ridiculed about something. What could the ridicule be?

If Mama engages in questionable activities and other parents know or suspect such things, how long will it take for your son to get into an altercation defending you, all without truly understanding **your** activity's ramifications? We all know, from our own childhood experiences, that kids are the cruelest! When a child says something vulgar to another kid, he heard or learned it from an adult. Could it be that your son knows far more than you think he knows about your activities and is either embarrassed about it or not interested in getting beat-down by a kid who confronts him with it?

Lies to the Son

Here's another situation:

> Your son tries to get into your room one morning
> when you are "busy" and you were forced to stop
> abruptly and get dressed (at least partially), what
> will he be thinking as he tries to enter your room?
> Will he be surprised or annoyed? An annoyance
> like, "You promised you would not do this
> anymore," type of disgust or surprised like, "I didn't
> know Mama did such things." If your reaction is,
> "Oh sh**, I cannot get caught doing *this* again!
> How will I explain this one?" Then your reaction
> says that such activities are common place and not
> the first time your being "caught in the act" has
> happened. Your making-up excuses and lying to
> your son, playing him for stupid about your sexual
> practices, **WILL** eventually backfire against you...
> and you know what? You will deserve it!

If such scenarios make you very uneasy... anxious
even, then you have a serious issue on your hands. Is
your anxiety stemming from what he THINKS about
you? How does he FEEL about you? More likely than
not, his *feelings* are that he simply loves you because

you are his mom! What he *thinks* of you… hmm? Which one is more important to you?

YOUR BOY AIN'T STUPID!

If you think by putting up that fake façade, you will prevent your son from knowing about your promiscuous behavior… it's too late. He knows more,

> *Falsehood is cowardice, the truth courage.*
> --Hosea Ballou

and has many more adverse opinions of you, than you think he does; he just may not know how to articulate or has not outwardly expressed them to you yet but don't worry, he will. The author is certain there is clear evidence of your behavior, to him, and a host of other things that you do. Trying (for the sake of your son) to look like you are a content happy mom (who is not getting [or trying to get] f#@*?% on the regular) is a lie. You need to let him know "how you roll" (Mama likes to f#@*… well, maybe not that crude but at least along the lines like: Mama likes the company of men… a lot!) and let the chips fall where they may. At least he will respect your up front honesty, if nothing else.

If your current activities make you like a [blank] and your past actions make you like a [blank] just accept the title and stop frontin' like you are something different, and besides that, you will feel 100 pounds lighter without the burden of acting like something you are not: a normal pristine mom, *married* to his father, before he was born, with no outside kids from the marriage.

GOT RESPECT?

Disrespect is not always a frontal attack. More often than not, it is in very subtle ways, whether you see it or not, and the disrespect **will** get worse. Telling him that sex is solely for procreation and not recreation, as he sees a half-naked man come out of his mother's bedroom, will make you look bad and erodes the respect factor. What was the half-naked man doing? Trying to make him a little brother or sister? Your boy ain't that stupid! As he gets older, and with every exposure to what a normal family structure looks like, he will compare it with the behavior his mother has exhibited, and is exhibiting, with men. Again, with each exposure of "normalcy," the worst his attitude and respect will become towards you. Most boys of Black Single Moms are angry. They are angry at the fact that their father is not in the household, and possibly their lives, while growing-up. That anger will, at times, be targeted towards you (Single Moms); whether he tells you so or not, he is blaming you on some level for the situation. As crazy as it may sound, if he ever sees you happy with a man and that man is not showing him that same level of attention then he will make a subconscious link, in his head. He will think, "Well, why couldn't she have done that with my dad?" Consciously, he will know why his mom is not with his father but subconsciously he is going to lay the blame on you, no matter what you say.

BEHAVIOR COMES FROM SOMEWHERE

If Mama is of low quality then guess what, with a 90% probability, the son will be of low quality too. The apple never falls far from the tree. When these so called, self-proclaimed, Black Advocates condemn various behaviors of young Black Males about their outwardly expressed attitude towards women **and** want it to cease, it has to make you LAUGH! When these advocates are told how to solve this problem, they do not want to hear the solution because **it cuts too close to home** (their own upbringing!). This

> *If the truth doesn't save us, what does that say about us?*
> --Lois McMaster Bujold

form of denial compels you to LAUGH EVEN HARDER because now they are just blowing hot air up our asses! The solution **starts** with Black Women DECIDING not to give birth to bastardized children. No one wants to acknowledge the ROOT of the problem but only the symptoms and wonder why things are on a continuous downward spiral! Where the f#@* do you think they got it from? How do you think it got started? They got it by watching their Mama! You may say, "What!" But check it out: What's a hoe? Very simply put, a woman who engages in promiscuous sexual behavior (with multiple, non-exclusive partners, during overlapping periods). What's a b*tch? It is a deprived woman with a bad attitude. What has he seen over the course of his childhood? His mom with (or damn sure knows about-it) multiple "companions." He also has seen her on edge (a b*tch) when she is not getting any "male attention." If she is sexually active, attractive and she is being deprived then she is going to be a b*tch! What do these Black Males call Black Women these days? Hoes and B*tches! Is it unfounded? Again, where do you think they got it? The older the Black Male Child becomes, growing up in a toxic environment, the less respect he has for her (subconsciously towards his mom) and a broad disrespect directed towards women as a whole. If this is the type of crap (the guy), in epidemic proportions, the Black Community is putting into a larger society then what do you expect? Mama had five opportunities to prevent this obscenity but CHOSE not to.

Black Women who decide to have bastard sons and continue their sexual behavior without missing a beat, are enormous contributors to why the Black Community is in its current state of decline. Until Black Women stop having bastard children, under the aforementioned conditions, you will continue to have an escalation in the crisis we are currently experiencing.

The power is in the hands of the Black Woman. The Black Community is responsible for its own destruction by allowing those circumstances to continue.

AGAIN, YOUR BOY AIN'T STUPID!

Promiscuous Single Moms, are you worried about your son? Don't be. He already knows about your behavior and is already desensitized, by the time he reaches his early teens, to seeing you with or knowing you are going out with, different men. For the Black Male Child, who has never seen his mother married to his father, every day of his life, this is common. The biggest fallacy of this whole ordeal is not the promiscuous behavior of Promiscuous Single Moms, it is that your sons see this as "normal." They *may* not have known when they were younger, as to what you were doing but they are extremely aware now. Sorry to break it to you, but the damage is done.

Too harsh on Mama? REALLY?!

Share your suggestions

AND

Produce some

solutions at:

MamasFAULT.com

CONTINUED PRACTICES

I never did give them hell. I just told the truth, and they thought it was hell.

–Harry S Truman

Chapter 5

CONTINUED PRACTICES

THE SEX CONTINUES

Now you got Mama with this son, still probably young, looks very attractive and still wants the company of a man that she may even want to marry. She, of course, is not going to find "the sucker" on the first outing she goes. In all probability, she is not going to abstain from sex while she is looking for "the sucker" to marry her either. She will inadvertently, or maybe even consciously, expose her son (if by nothing more than her demeanor, attitude, moods, focus, etc.) to between 5 – 8 men (if not more) over the course of his childhood. Some sluts will do that within any given 6 to 10 month period! The author is unequivocally certain that you know one or two females that fit that description right now!

REPUTATIONS SPREAD

How many of us know women who wear tight shorts, very revealing clothing or blouses with no bra, while relaxing in the privacy of their own home? Everyone, right? Okay, now picture them in that same type of garb, walking around in public. What would be your opinion of that woman, whether right or wrong, if they admitted that they did/do it to attracted the attention of men? How many Black Single Moms actually parade around like that, dangling themselves out to see what they can catch? How many of these women's neighbors, co-workers and those in various social circles know about such actions?

Guys talk, just like women. A guy will say or do what's on his mind (especially when he is inebriated), BASED UPON, what he has been told by other guys. Just as women will tell other women about how inadequate, small, limp, "15 second man!" etc. guys are, guys will talk along similar lines too. Guys will talk about what various acts females are eager to do (straight f#@*\!$, sucking d***, back-door, threesome, etc.) and if it was worth whatever it took to get it! Guys will talk about where those females do it, where they hang out and when you can find them. Guys will even talk about what you have to do (or bring along) once you catch-up with them (money, drugs, food, alcohol, just be nice, whatever!). The point is this: Nothing happens by accident. The author will say it over and over again, "If it walks like a [blank] and talks like a [blank] then the author will bet even money that it is a [blank]." When women are labeled with promiscuous reputations, whether they are aware of it or not, the

> *Not being known doesn't stop the truth from being true.*
> --Richard Bach

recovery from such depths is steep. This is all to say that the son will eventually pick-up on, if not already told by his peer group, the reputation his Mama carries.

GOTTA HAVE IT

What is a nymphomaniac? In layman's terms, it is a girl addicted to sex.

Sometime in 2007-2008, the author watched a movie on cable, "Black Snake Moan," starring Samuel L. Jackson. In the movie, the girl's boyfriend (played by Justin Timberlake) went into the military, leaving her alone. She just had to have sex, all the time, and drugs if available, to escape her pain. The question that comes to mind is this: why did she suffer such an affliction? As the movie progressed, it became clear how she became that way; it was the way in which she was raised (or lack of) and exposure to adverse circumstances.

In 2008, the author saw another movie but this time in theaters, "Sex in the City: The Movie" and paid particular attention to the character played by Kim Catrail. In one of the scenes, someone in the theater mentioned something to the effect of cutting her sex down to 3-4 days a week. It got a laugh out of me but there were those in the theater who cheered, saying something to the effect of, "I'd be upset too girl!"

In healthy *exclusive* relationships, having sex is important, to most couples. However, when sex is perverted into a woman flipping through her proverbial "Black Book" to f#@*, or get f#@*?%, it brings into question a woman's character. For those in the audience screaming that guys do it all the time, the author admits that you are right! Yes, it is a double standard, but this book is about what women do to psychologically damage the Male Child **not** what guys do.

As the author said in an earlier section, the sons of Black Single Moms are not stupid! Whether their moms are getting f#@*?% at the house or creeping late hours in the street, they know what mom is doing. Now, what they call women who exhibit that type of behavior... well, the author has some choice terms. What do you think they call them?

THE SIGNS ARE POSTED

Trial balloons are what you send-up during the midst of a conversation to test whether or not the concept, which you are mentioning, is acceptable. The author had an experience where he was asked if he had ever dated multiple women, with whom he had sexual relations, while seeing all of them during the same period (month, quarter, etc.): A Man Whore, if-you-will. **Not realizing it then**, the woman who asked me the question was in essence telling me that she engages in that type of behavior and was trying to gage my acceptance or disgust of the issue. Of course, *her engaging* in that type of behavior would disgust me but the author did not recognize *the sign* right away.

There were three distinct occurrences that made it REALLY clear to him that the author was amongst a multitude of different guys in which she was f#@*\!$ for all types of reasons! This in-of-itself is bad but when you factor in the fact that she was *playing* the "pristine mom" role to a pre-teen boy... that tragedy expands ten-fold.

LET'S CALL IT WHAT IT IS!

All great truths begin as blasphemies.

–GEORGE BERNARD SHAW

Chapter 6

LET'S CALL IT WHAT IT IS!

WHAT'S YOUR DEFINITION?

No intelligent, self-respecting man wants a slut/whore for his woman and he damn sure is not going to marry one, with a bastard child as a constant reminder of what she is, unless...! What is **your** definition of this type of woman?

The author's definition of a whore is a woman who engages in sexual acts, with multiple, non-exclusive partners, during overlapping periods, even if considered exclusive to one of the partners. Simply put, *they* have sexual relations with numerous men (the reason does not matter: horny, loneliness, hurt, revenge, the guy she usually has sex with is inadequate, money, just because, whatever!). Question: With how many **NON-EXCLUSIVE** partners did "the female in question" have sexual relations with, in the last 12 months alone (four, six, eight), not to include prior months/years?

If this has been a woman's behavior, what other designation would you give her? If she is not getting rich then the name will be SLUT. A *true* whore gets rich, a slut just gets f#@*?%... pun extremely intended (f#@*?% over to be precise).

WHAT'S IN A NAME?

A slut and a whore are one in the same in that they f#@* & suck, numerous men! More accurately: a woman who engages in sexual acts, with multiple, non-exclusive partners, during overlapping periods, even if considered exclusive to one of the partners (sucker). That is where the similarities end.

To note the differences between a cheap slut and an expensive whore, we must determine where she stands. In Chart 1 below, you will find those variations, as you move from the lower left to the upper right, based on the characteristics of a slut versus a whore.

CHART 1 - COST DIFFERENCES

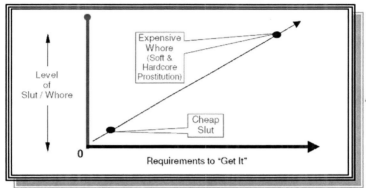

The vertical axis charts the "level of slut / whore." This represents the *value* of the hoe more so than their social / economic standing. The horizontal axis is a function of what the guy has to offer via material possessions, favors, intellect, physically and in cases of the varying forms of prostitution, financial resources.

THE SLUT

The slut f#@*~ & sucks because they just like to do it, she's just "gotta have it" and it does not cost the guy anything, hence the definition: a cheap slut! She may be f#@*\!$ someone new every-other-week (if given an opportunity) based on superficial trivialities, the way a guy looks or that the other men she usually "does" are not available. The guys that get their d**** sucked and are f#@*?% by them, are there for just that and if they can get anything extra, well, that is just a bonus. No man of substance is going to want trifling trash for his woman (no matter what she has [house, car, etc] or can do for him [cook, buy him things, etc.]), when he knows (or finds out) she *likes to* f#@* & suck other guys and has a reputation for doing so. Even so, it is not surprising that most sluts become emotionally attached to the d**** they suck (pun intended), probably because it is the only way and time they can get guys to pay them any undivided attention. Further more, most sluts are not even smart enough to figure out why a guy, even without substance, does not want to be committed to a-piece-of-ass that has f#@*?% multiple guys in a short period (i.e. at least 8 different guys | 90 day period); not smart enough to figure out that you cannot

> *Wisdom is found only in truth.*
> --Johann Wolfgang von Goethe

find love at the end of a guy's d***! If she must have a man, there is a bright spot in a slut's life in that the same type of guy who would marry a woman with kids would also marry a slut. Eventually, the slut gets a clue and decides to become a whore. Although not a *true* whore, she finally realizes that if she is going to be considered trash, and is compelled to suck d*** anyway, she might as well get something out of it... or at least try to.

THE WHORE

The *true* whore is unemotional and looking to get something tangible out of the exchange and not, like the slut, just out to have sex. When this occurs, we move into Soft Prostitution. The whore is not necessarily f#@*\!$-for-fun but to get things done! She is a little bit more discrete and does between 2 – 3 guys, at any point-in-time, to get "things" taken care of. The *true* whore is willing to stomach f#@*\!$ almost any guy who has the means of getting her what she wants. This is usually not a problem since there are a number of guys at nightspots stupid enough to take care of those needs in exchange for sex; the places where low quality women meet low quality guys.

YOU'RE TO GOOD TO BE AN AMATEUR

Whether a man or woman, you may be able to learn something from this personal interaction submitted below. If you are a man and this happens to you then you may be dealing with a female who ain't your typical "girl next door" type! If you are a woman and you exhibit this type of behavior then now you know why the guy is treating you the way he is.

The guy wrote:

> During our first sexual encounter, when she wanted to "do me" after I "did her," I asked that she didn't. She told me that it was important to her and that it was something she **really** liked to do (that cracked open "the box") and that it was part of **her** fulfillment. She also said it would help my endurance. Wait! How would she know that sucking a guy's d*** would improve his endurance!? She could only know that if it is a practice of hers. In this case, she would get two bonuses: something she **really** likes to do, sucking their d**** AND getting f#@*?% longer! I guess you can't beat that!
>
> Also during our first encounter, she did something that gave herself away as to her normal practices. **BEFORE** we got started, she went upstairs and got two condoms. Okay, she wants to practice safe sex but no, it was more to it than that. One was a normal lubricated condom and the other one was **MINT FLAVORED**! The only reason a girl uses a flavored condom is if she is planning on sucking his

d***!! It is what she uses when she is not familiar with a guy's sexual history; her first time sucking *his* d***, which it would have been. If this was not enough, the condom she gave me to use had an expiration date of 2005, which meant that she had to purchase the pack in '03 or '04 (if not before!). With, or without flavored condoms, she has been sucking d**** on the regular for quite a while, "no matter what *she said* she doesn't do *often*."

On a separate encounter, made tremendously clear again, as to what she **really** likes to do, was when she told me, "This ain't about you, it's what I want to do." (that blew the lid off "the box"). I think it's logical to conclude that she likes sucking d****, no matter what *she said* she doesn't do *often*.

Even clearer still was when she did me twice one morning, when I insisted she did not. She said jokingly (but I am sure on some level she believed there was some element of truth to it), and I am paraphrasing, "You already think I'm a whore so **I might as well do what I like to do!**" When she told me this, it was no wonder why guys have talked and treated her like sh** (her prior experience with *other* men) since that is what guys do with sluts; their purpose is for f#@*\!$. If she thinks, I think, she is a whore (well, actually a slut) then God knows guys of lesser intellectual capacity MUST think that of her, pick-up on it and pursue her as such! There is no way any woman, with half a sense, could think otherwise about that perception.

Jeff --

To the Women reading this story, is this how you want to be seen? The author would suspect, IT IS NOT!

Fellas, in relation to the above story, have you ever had a female tell you, "I don't *do that....*"? What does that mean? Translation: that is exactly what she does!

Women, do not tell a man what it is that you do not do. Just don't do it! Let your actions speak for themselves not your mouth (you decide if there is a pun intended).

The story below (again, submitted by a man) is a perfect example of how foolish a woman can look lying about what it is that she doesn't do, all in an effort to get what she wants.

A female told me, "I must really like a guy first before I suck his d***." I knew this was Bull Sh** because of a previous conversation when she told me about a situation involving a radio personality:

> She claimed she was ready to go suck and/or f#@* him just after midnight. If he would have called before she went to sleep around 4am, she would have been there to not only give him some head but to probably also literally "take one in the a**," all to not mess-up a future business opportunity with this guy! Unbeknown to her, I knew the story was bogus and that she had already f#@*?% him, probably the same night I met her, if not months before. One of the radio personality's Fraternity Brothers, that I knew, that she didn't know that I knew, spoke to me after he saw me speaking with her at a particular Fundraiser Brunch. He told me about the two of them and gave me the 411 about her freaky-a**, which I suspected but didn't really know at the time.

Because I never told this female about what I knew, a similar situation happened again! The point here is that if patterns emerge, there is no denying what you are working with.

> The same type of scenario and she didn't miss a beat! A guy she knows from out-of-town, has something she really wants (like the Radio

Let's Call It What It Is!

Personality!). He's only going to be here a short while but is just so busy, all day long, that he can only see her at a very late hour (just like the Radio Personality!), to give her what she needs, after he gets what he wants. Sound familiar? Now, the previous day, this producer blew her off (no pun intended) at 11pm then at 1am until she got tired of waiting and went to bed around 4am (just like the Radio Personality scenario, minus the calling at 11pm then at 1am!). Lucky for her, this out-of-town producer was here for one more day! This time, once again, she waited on the couch (I guess to get her head together for what she was about to do) for that phone call and when it came through, she was out the door... "to take care of some business." She was going to do WHATEVER it took to get those music tracks and "take one in the a** (or do one)" for the team!

After these two incidents, there could be no denying in my mind that she could, and I'm sure she still does, disassociate herself from the sexual act if it is for some type of justifiable gain in her head. I'm convinced that she will rationalize away the performing of any act as somehow having been right and acceptable under the circumstances she faces and sees absolutely nothing wrong with it. Yea, she is a Single Mom and sorry to say that she reflects badly on the *FEW* who do not subscribe to such practices of "whatever it takes."

Will --

When a woman's only "standard" for sucking a guy's d*** is that he can do something for her (financially or do her a favor) **OR** that he looks attractive enough, to her, to f#@* we got a serious character flaw here!

Dr. Dré (a recording artist) has this track, "Housewife" on his "2001" CD. One of the versus says:

> "...the way she was blowing, I know she does it a lot..." and the hook goes: "...so what you found a hoe that you like, you can't make a hoe a housewife..."

> *Truth is meant to save you first, and the comfort comes afterward.*
> --Georges Bernanos

This is all to say that there is no way a woman can be that good, enjoy it that much and NOT do it that often, to a number of guys. The author GUARANTEES YOU that if their son(s) knew what their Mama does/did with her lips, they would not want to be kissing their mom-the-slut. The author will take that bet anytime that anybody is ready.

WHAT EVERY GUY DOESN'T WANT

There is a difference between f#@*\!$ a slut and having a slut as your woman. Deny it all you want but even married guys secretly (or outwardly admit to it) want, or like, to f#@* sluts, because there is just something supposedly exciting about it! This goes without saying, every man wants a freak in the bedroom: a woman who can f#@* & suck like a pro but if he cannot get it from his "significant other" then some men will get it from a slut on the side! However, no *intelligent* man, or even the dumb-a**-loser, wants a slut for his woman, as the mother of his son and damn sure not his wife (but may settle for if desperate enough)! No man **wants** to know, or anyone else to find out, about all the other guys his woman has had sexual relations with and especially coming in contact with, and learning about, them while she is having relations with him! No intelligent man is under the delusion that his woman has not been with other guys, so that is not the issue. He just does not what to be reminded of her past (or maybe even current history) behaviors, **evident by her present actions**. If she goes to the same "suspect" places, continues to communicate with the same low grade people then he is going to learn very quickly about what she "used to do" (or probably is still doing!). He is going to learn very quickly about the quality of her character by observing her female & male associations (birds-of-a-feather) and their interactions. Guys talk, just as women do, reputations spread fast and the truth will ALWAYS surface! No man wants to be the butt of jokes about his having a slut, or a whore, as his woman.

What a woman does in the initial days, weeks or the month of "seeing" a guy is indicative of what she does on a regular basis. This is the period where she sets the precedent for how the rest of the relationship plays out. If a woman allows a guy to f#@* her, and particularly if she sucks his d***, before they are 100% confident that the two are exclusive to each other then that sends up a red flag. An act that **any** guy, with any knowledge of women, will ALWAYS remember AND in the negative. A guy is not going to say to himself, "Wow! I got a *private freak*." Naaa! It is going to be more like, "If she's sucking my d***, and we have not openly expressed 100% exclusivity to each other, then she's f#@*\!$ & sucking other guys the same way too!" In guy terms, that's a trifling slut! Again, most guys do not have a problem f#@*\!$ sluts, it is just that **most** intelligent guys are not dumb enough to allow those "relations" to progress to the point of a real "relationship."

A female who allows herself to become, or show that she can be, a nasty hoe BEFORE the commitment, can forget about keeping any man, of any remote indicators of substance and quality around long-term. If by chance, AFTER THE FACT, a woman begins to develop an emotional attachment to the guy and now believes a guy is exclusive and/or committed to her (because she f#@*?% & sucked him in the first month, heaven forbid the first week) then she has some serious delusional psychological issues (a "Night Club Hoe" mentality)! Her process is backwards and any female that does this deserves what she gets! Again, what do you expect from women who hangout at bars and clubs? A guy knows what he has (if she sucks his d*** without exclusivity) and the category ain't marrying material; she is put into the category of "d*** sucking sluts on the side" because you cannot make a hoe into a housewife. Once a woman opens that door, the author guarantees you, an intelligent guy will ALWAYS remember that past and she cannot go back and change it later.

What's for Sale?

There are few nudities so objectionable as the naked truth.

−Agnes Repplier

Chapter 7

WHAT'S FOR SALE?

EXHIBIT 1 – Degrees of Prostitution

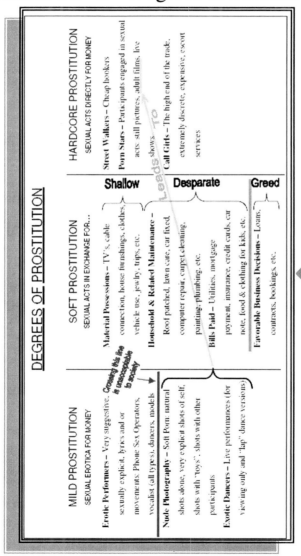

DEGREES OF PROSTITUTION

MILD PROSTITUTION
SEXUAL EROTICA FOR MONEY

Erotic Performers – Very suggestive, sexually explicit, lyrics and or movements. Phone Sex Operators, vocalist (all types), dancers, models

Crossing this line is unacceptable to society

Nude Photography – Soft Porn: natural shots alone, very explicit shots of self, shots with "toys", shots with other participants

Exotic Dancers – Live performances (for viewing only and "lap" dance versions)

SOFT PROSTITUTION
SEXUAL ACTS IN EXCHANGE FOR...

Material Possessions – TV's, cable connection, house furnishings, clothes, vehicle use, jewelry, trips, etc.

Household & Related Maintenance – Roof patched, lawn care, car fixed computer repair, carpet cleaning, painting, plumbing, etc.

Bills Paid – Utilities, mortgage payment, insurance, credit cards, car note, food & clothing for kids, etc.

Favorable Business Decisions – Loans, contracts, bookings, etc.

Shallow

Desparate

Greed

Leads To

HARDCORE PROSTITUTION
SEXUAL ACTS DIRECTLY FOR MONEY

Street Walkers – Cheap hookers

Porn Stars – Participants engaged in sexual acts: still pictures, adult films, live shows

Call Girls – The high end of the trade. extremely discrete, expensive, escort services

PROSTITUTION

Contrary to popular belief, prostitution is not only straight sex for money but other variations too. Prostitution can run from being very mild, to soft, to hardcore. Mild Prostitution is usually always public, Soft Prostitution is usually private and Hardcore Prostitution can be either publicly displayed or private.

MILD PROSTITUTION

Personal performances done with a sexual implication is Sexual Erotica. When done for money, it is also known as Mild Prostitution (see the corresponding heading in Exhibit 1 or the Blow-up in this section). This type can be private (visual identity of the performer masked) or very public. Performances considered Mild Prostitution are those which only contribute to the targeted audience's arousal through suggestion but are not engaging in the sexual act. Several forms range from simple erotic poetry up to "lap" dances, which can come within literally millimeters of conducting a sexual act. Although today's society is begrudgingly accepting of exhibitionists display of public sexuality, through entertainment (and perhaps may even giggle at it), the line is universally crossed when that sexuality involves nudity and notably when it is for money.

EROTIC PERFORMERS

The language in various forms of music and poetry are some of the more tolerant forms of Mild Prostitution and are very public; most people just blow it off as harmless while still other groups want to censor it. Everybody knows that SEX

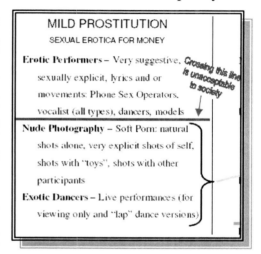

MILD PROSTITUTION
SEXUAL EROTICA FOR MONEY

Erotic Performers – Very suggestive, sexually explicit, lyrics and or movements: Phone Sex Operators, vocalist (all types), dancers, models

Crossing this line is unacceptable to society

Nude Photography – Soft Porn: natural shots alone, very explicit shots of self, shots with "toys", shots with other participants

Exotic Dancers – Live performances (for viewing only and "lap" dance versions)

SELLS or at least, in these cases, the suggestion of such does. The performers may wear sexually suggestive clothing and recite very explicit material but, as in all sexual erotica, their performance does not include performing the sexual act... at least not in that public setting! There is a strong correlation between the success of the erotic artist and the display of that sex appeal, during erotic performances and off stage in public. The greater the amount of public exposure that they can produce through whatever means possible, the greater number of followers a performer can capture. The quality of character of such performers is always at question simply due to the fact of the material they perform. No, they are not performing sexual acts directly for favors or money, as in the other forms of prostitution, but they are not abstaining from its suggestion either.

Phone sex operators are considered to be performing Mild Prostitution. They are paid to keep the caller on the line as long as possible or for them to call back very frequently in order to make money. They do so by using very, very sexually explicit language and tonality to get and keep the caller excited. Although the performer generally speaks to anyone from the public, their true identity remains private. The joke is that the appearance of the performer is nothing like what you imagine them to look like. In fact, if you were to see most of them you would become unexcited very quickly!

What's for Sale?

NUDE PHOTOGRAPHY

"Crossing the Line" into Soft Porn and Nudity, available for **anyone** to see, is unacceptable to polite society. If at any point you doubt this statement, just ask the question as to whether or not you would want your children to see it. If the answer is no then it is not acceptable to polite society (defined as the public) as a whole. It comes down to a moral issue and that the display of ones nudity is for the private pleasures of ones "significant other." The only intent of Soft Porn is to induce sexual arousal, its production is for sale to the public and calls into question the displayed individuals' *total* character. The nude photos can range from a model in just natural positions (standing, sitting, etc.), to extremely suggestive sexual positions. The more explicit and suggestive the poses the model can strike, the more money she can make. She may introduce sex toys into various orifices or shot with other participants "assisting" or touching, without actually performing the sexual act. However, all too often, such photo shoots will progress (or have in the past) into actual sexual acts on camera. Whether shot in natural positions or with other participants and props, polite society will label such a person as a bona fide whore regardless.

PHOTOS - INNOCENT TO EXPLICIT IN A FLASH

Have you ever seen nude pictures of what most people would call an attractive women and wonder, how in the world did they ever get those girls to take those photos? Well, it is a process on the part of the photographer and the past conditioning of the target throughout their life. Soft Porn and Nudity: let's see how it could start and where it can and most likely end-up.

➢ **Candid** Shots – Innocent amateur Polaroids or snap shots in a casual setting, in causal clothing.

➢ **Elegant** Shots – She eventually starts posing for photos with full make-up and in something elegant.

➢ **Tight Clothing** Shots – Clothes very tight and showing very little skin. Possibly a tight dress to overstate her total body curvature or a tight blouse to show off her breast. For the bottom, a pair of skintight jeans or the pants from a suit; something that follows the contours of her butt, hips, thighs and crotch.

➢ **Skin Revealing** Shots – Tightly contoured clothing and revealing a lot of skin (the "slut uniform"). Something you probably would not wear to church; then again, in black churches… A low cut, tight blouse to show, and push-up, cleavage; a short skirt to see her legs and tight panties; an open back stopping just above her butt.

➢ **Swimsuit** - Regular 2 piece, supportive set. Something you would actually see worn and used at a pool. Shots taken in various respectable positions and a few teasing shots of her taking off her top, and doing the same with the bottom, but not fully exposing her breast, butt or crotch.

➢ **Semi-Nudes** - Shots in clothing anyone could see through or those taken in extremely skimpy outfits. During the same session, she may also do shots in swimsuits that amount to nothing more than strings and fabric, barely covering her nipples and private spot.

➢ **Full Nudes** – From "Semi-Nudes," or any of the other starts, a photographed female's initial nude shots may be very mild: T & A in normal positions. As she becomes increasingly comfortable, the photos end-up becoming freakier and freakier. After a few, or numerous, separate Nude shoots, the only thing left is performing sexual acts in movies.

PHOTOS - ONLY ONE REAL REASON

Why does a woman take Nude Photos? It is one of three reasons or all. One, the photographer has appealed to their low self-esteem; Two, the photographer speaks of how great they will look "modeling" for him and/or; Three, financial gain. More than likely, it is the later. Not financial gain? What will she do with these photos, keep them for her private collection? No, she is going to show the photos to somebody and it ain't gonna be just to her boyfriend. She will sell this sexual erotica to someone, somewhere, in order to make money; also know as Mild Prostitution, which, as mentioned earlier, officially puts her into the bona fide whore category.

What's for Sale?

PHOTOS - THE OPPOSITE OF TASTEFUL

The author has heard the argument, many times, that such acts were done for artistic purposes! Artistic Value?! Will she display the photos in an Art Museum or will they be in someone's private porno collection? The author thinks the porno collection so that negates the "Artistic Value" Bull-Sh**! Will she pay the photographer and take all the shots and negatives with her or will the photographer pay her and retain all the rights? If the later, f#@* the artistic bull-sh**, AGAIN, it's porn! Regardless of who owns the rights, the purposes of a woman's nude photos are to arouse guys (women in some cases!) in order to "serve" themselves or function as an aphrodisiac with a partner. When a woman says *her* nude photos are for artistic purposes, who the f#@* is fooling who? Is she trying to fool herself or everyone else into believing that what she did was not tasteless.

PHOTOS - CONSEQUENCES ARE CERTAIN

A number of women are, at various times in their lives, convinced that the "sex trade," in all of its forms, is some how okay to get involved in. You hear it all the time: I need a little money to pay for school; It's the only job I can get that pays money above minimum wage; I have a family to support; etc., etc. etc. **VERY** few of these women ever think of the consequences that will inevitably come if they ever make it out of the toxic environment they DECIDE to work.

The author, of course, does not know what the LONG-TERM intentions are with women of such character but it sure is not going to be in anything of substance if their current actions are of any indication. No matter what agreements they had with the photographers, those will not be worth-a-damn, if the woman becomes successful or even comes close. Those pictures they claim to have so much artistic value will surface and when they do, they will f#@*-up **anything of substance** they had going on. No legitimate business is going to want anything to do with that sh**. Artistic Value? When a guy sees a women who posses for such photos, his lips will not be forming anything close to the word artistic. The author would like women to think also of the look on their sons' faces when their photos *eventually* do hit the Internet! By the time they do, the son may be so f#@*?%-up that the viewing would not have much of an impact any way!

EXOTIC DANCERS

Nude Dancing qualifies as Mild Prostitution because of the nudity and the movements simulating the sexual act: the freakier the dancing, the more money a stripper can make. This is the most intense form of Mild Prostitution and can come literally within millimeters of performing the act, as with the case of "lap" dances. Most strippers just Strip and go on about their lives after leaving work. Others, however, take it to another level in that they cross over into Direct Prostitution or some eventually end up participating in Adult Films.

SOFT PROSTITUTION

Sexual acts in exchange for [whatever] is Soft Prostitution (see the corresponding heading in Exhibit 1 or the Blow-up to follow). It is the most deceptive form of prostitution in that it can be easily shrugged off as a female just having casual sex, basically just a slut again, or that it is her boyfriend. The difference between Soft Prostitution and being a slut is: Number 1 - this type of whore is getting

SOFT PROSTITUTION

SEXUAL ACTS IN EXCHANGE FOR...

Material Possessions – TV's, cable connection, house furnshings, clothes, vehicle use, jewlry, trips, etc.

Household & Related Maintenance – Roof patched, lawn care, car fixed, computer repair, carpet cleaning, painting, plumbing, etc.

Bills Paid – Utilities, mortgage payment, insurance, credit cards, car note, food & clothing for kids, etc.

Favorable Business Decisions – Loans, contracts, bookings, etc.

Shallow

Desparate

Greed

something in exchange for a sexual act(s), whereas the slut is just getting f#@*?% and; Number 2 - she is getting something in exchange for the sexual act(s) from **more than one guy**, not just a boyfriend. Let's define boyfriend here for a second: A boyfriend is exclusive to girlfriend! What a concept… right?! NOT: a boyfriend defined as ONE OF THE MANY d**** she sucks! A title she gives in order to avoid looking like the crap that she is!

No matter what you call her, a Slut or Prostitute, neither title seems favorable. Soft Prostitution can be as subtle as the female saying, "I have something for you *after* you fix my computer," to being very direct where a person in power insist on getting f#@*?% and/or sucked *before* approving a business decision in the whore's favor. This type of whore is out to acquire something and her currency is the sexual act. This is the type of whore that will walk into a bar, as an example, with the expressed intent of (and probably the invoice too!), "I'm going to get this electric bill paid!" When a woman has, in cases that pertain to Soft Prostitution, financial challenges stemming from being a single parent, having little or no education, inadequate income, depleted savings and weak moral values she is going to resort to these tactics. Think not? The author highly suggests that you think again… a little harder!

MATERIAL POSSESSIONS

Whoring for material possessions is the shallowest of the Soft Prostitution categories. Considered the shallowest type of whore because the items obtained represent nothing of absolute need. A woman may not specifically seek material possessions but when the opportunity to get them presents itself, she may not have a problem making "an exchange." This is also the same type of whore that: probably lacks the intellectual capacity (reflected in her lack of education) to earn a substantial living, is lacking the moral character to not whore herself out and has too many

> *The truth is incontrovertible, malice may attack it, ignorance may deride it but in the end, there it is!*
> --Winston Churchill

trivial expenditures (hair, nails, eating out, etc.) that exhausts the little money she does have for more important matters like food for her bastard son. She finds herself in predicaments where she needs a few things done, or maybe a little cash, and provides men with a "favor," or two.

HOUSEHOLD & RELATED MAINTENANCE

Household & related maintenance issues come up a lot for single woman, markedly those in Single Family Residences (houses not apartments). Countless things can go wrong in a house and she just may not have the ability to apply a temporary patch, completely repair or upgrade the item or situation. If task or things around the house require maintenance and she does not have the financial resources to render timely solutions then she will do "an exchange" to have those things handled in the appropriate manner.

What's for Sale?

BILLS PAID

Not getting bills paid could have the most harmful effect, out of the Soft Prostitution categories, on a woman and notably one with children. While not getting household maintenance done is an inconvenience, not having a place to live can be devastating, in an extreme case of not being able to pay the rent/mortgage. At this point, a woman who has never "sold" her body or compromised her integrity **may begin** to do so in these cases. If not righted quickly, the habit can easily become a way of life.

FAVORABLE BUSINESS DECISIONS

Sex in exchange for favorable business decisions; Whoring at its finest! However, this "gray line" does not really need to be crossed. While not tending to bills paid and household maintenance can have harsh consequences, not landing a business deal, based on its own merits, is not of the same urgency. Resorting to sexual favors is a matter of greed and the pride of achieving an undertaking without asking for that assistance from friends, family or colleagues! Although possibly the most lucrative actions of a whore, it speaks very poorly of the woman's character if she has to stoop to such levels to push a business action through. It says that she is operating from some low self-esteem and not very confident in what she is selling, since it cannot stand on its own merits. It may be easy for the author to say no business deal is worth all that but it may be an entirely different issue for a shallow minded, greedy whore desperate to prove she can survive on her own.

HARDCORE PROSTITUTION

Hardcore Prostitution is the type that is most noted by the public (see the corresponding heading in Exhibit 1 or the Blow-up below). People envision hookers walking up and down busy avenues and standing on the street corners of destitute neighborhoods. Although there are slight variations to this form of prostitution, the basis is the same: They perform sexual acts, all types of ways, **directly**

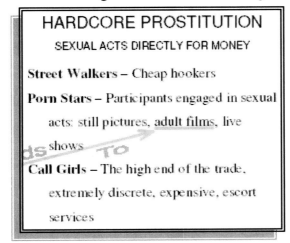

HARDCORE PROSTITUTION

SEXUAL ACTS DIRECTLY FOR MONEY

Street Walkers – Cheap hookers

Porn Stars – Participants engaged in sexual acts: still pictures, adult films, live shows

Call Girls – The high end of the trade, extremely discrete, expensive, escort services for money. The differences lie in the level of discretion and exposure.

STREET WALKERS

The Street Walker, otherwise known as a filthy rotten whore, will perform any sexual act, on anybody, as long as the "customer" has the money she request. They use very little discretion and will perform the sexual act anywhere that is convenient. Street prostitution is very widespread, considered a public nuisance, and deemed illegal in all 50 states except Nevada. It is easy to discern who is selling what by the manner in which the whore is "marketing" herself in the street; she is usually wearing the "slut uniform." The marketing is public but the sexual act takes place in private or at least away from law enforcement officials.

PORN STARS

Hard Porn is the largest, and most commercialized, part of the multi-billion dollar sex industry: The sexual act performed in Adult Films and on still photos. There are even clubs that feature live sex shows performed on stage settings. In Hard Porn, the performer is very public for the masses to see. In fact, that is the objective; for them to be a "star!" A "porn star," more precisely. Depending on the influence of the pro, they may have some discretion over which pro(s) they will work with.

Many times for fun, amateurs perform for the camera, in photographs and in movies. There may be some compensation but they are not doing it for a living. It may be along the lines of something they are doing with a boyfriend or out of desperation to pay a bill.

CALL GIRLS

Call Girls are very discrete prostitutes. These women carry a very high price and are available to high-end clientele who require "dates" periodically to various functions. As elegant as she may appear to the outside, this whore is all about business, a lucrative business. The more exclusive she is to a client, the more expensive she becomes to keep: The Pay-to-Stay arrangement.

What's for Sale?

MOVIES ARE A STEP AWAY

As the author mentioned earlier in the chapter, a "conditioning" process takes place over time, a process that goes from the innocent to the explicit. None of this *just* happens! The submitted story below is an example of how a female could go from nude photos to movies.

> One afternoon, my very new girlfriend and I were in the kitchen preparing dinner at her house. She began asking me questions about some of my interest and how I would react to various situations. One of the questions was in reference to porno and if I watch it. She asked me a series of questions from what race to how I would watch it (internet, rentals, pay-per-view) and if I would watch it with her. She went on to say which types of porn she didn't like because it seemed dirty to her. I didn't interrupt her while she was speaking but I knew that what she was saying wasn't quite true. When I told her that I had seen some but not into it, the questions stopped.
>
> It seemed to me that she was very comfortable watching porn and did quite-a-bit of it before I came along. One night, I was extremely tired from work and unfortunately for me, and I guess her too, I had to go in the next day

on an earlier shift. Needless to say, I had to turn-in early if I had any chance of being productive in the morning. When I "showed no interest," her dissatisfaction became evident to me when, in the middle of the night, she went downstairs; it was to watch a porno! I let you figure out what she was doing while watching it!

A week before my girlfriend told me about her liking to watch porn, I saw a really nice professionally done photo of her she had in a frame. Jokingly, I commented, "Okay, now I want to see the rest of the set when you were nude!" To my surprise, she complied, as if it was nothing!

I knew she was a very sexual girl and aware of her sexual history. She's already posed nude in front of photographers (term used loosely), engaged in numerous sexual acts with multiple partners and she knows exactly what to do given the number of porno movies she has enjoyed watching for God knows how long. I also know about a couple of her friends who exhibit all of the signs of being **really** kinky and of whom I am certain have done some porno flicks at one time or another! Without question, my girl likes to fuck!

From her nude pics and watching porno, to her performing sexual acts on camera, it doesn't seem like a far leap for her to make. As much as I hate to admit it, I think she already has and got paid for it. A move, again, which I don't think was a big step for her.

Andy --

IT WILL ALWAYS BE WITH US

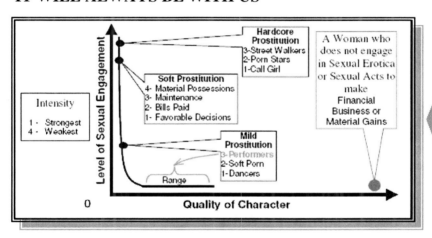

CHART 2 - CHARACTER

As noted throughout this chapter of the book, sexual behavior can take many forms. Noted since the beginning of time, the thought of being called a slut, whore, prostitute or whatever you want to call the female, has a negative connotation attached to a woman's Quality of Character (see Chart 2). Depending on how a female was raised, AND subsequent reference groups during childhood and currently, will determine if such a title is actually an insult. It is clear, by the author's observations, to many of the females with the aforementioned profiles, it is not.

The Wrong Stuff

Anger so clouds the mind, that it cannot perceive the truth.

–Cato the Elder
(234 BC - 149 BC)

Chapter 8

THE WRONG STUFF

DIFFERENT VALUE & BELIEF SYSTEMS

During the author's upbringing, the very THOUGHT of bringing a bastard child into the world was (and still is) reprehensible not to mention actually following through with it! The way in which **SOME** women bring children into the world is what really does not sit well with him. It is one thing to be a single mom, after 15 - 20 years of marriage and children all from the same father. It is an entirely different issue when you have never married but still decided to have a son anyway. It conveys a number of negative inferences about how a woman was raised, what she deems as acceptable and what inevitably will be taught (consciously or subconsciously) to the child while growing-up. At the end of the day, no matter how anyone slices it, the fact that a child is born will never change; it is irrevocable! The child will be a constant reminder of a woman's imbedded values. Other men, with similar backgrounds, may find this acceptable but the author ain't one of them!

Most boys in this type of household have a multi-year deficit of a strong consistent paternal example in the household that **A WOMAN** cannot make-up and with every passing year, **SHE** is making it worse. If the only examples and advice a woman is getting is coming from people who themselves got bastard children then that advice ain't worth sh**! Do you think the author is off-base? If so, just ask any 100 prospective men of substance, men with a future (not the losers discussed in Chapter 2), if they would take on the responsibility of raising another man's son; **ESPECIALLY when** it was from a mistake she will not even admit she has made. Because this is probably the only type of environment that a woman in such a position frequents, the author cannot be mad at her. These are the only type of people she associates with, on a regular basis, and cannot see (not even for a second) the detrimental effect of her actions; how her actions correlate to the failures in the Black Community, as a whole, by putting the results of another *fatherless* Black Male into society.

IF BROKE THEN FIX IT!

How do you rectify the position of a wayward bastard son, born to a Single Mom? Well, in actuality, you do not. IT'S DONE but for the sake of argument, what actions do you take to put that son of a Single Mom on the right path? How do you make-up for all those absent years of a strong consistent paternal figure, **SHE** did not provide in advance of the birth? First, **she** has

> *The truth will set you free. But first, it will p*ss you off.*
> --Gloria Steinem

to acknowledge what has happened. Once **she** accepts TOTAL responsibility for the debacle then she can get to a place where feasible solutions can work. Hold-up! Let's just stop right here! What are the chances of a Single Mom, emanating from over the last 50 years, taking full responsibility for her actions? Yea, right, the author does not see that happening! Not in a **Black Female** ran household! "It wasn't my fault and who needs that d*mn man anyway... right?" The author also hears it all the time of Single Moms constantly exclaiming just how happy they are for *their* son being born, which subconsciously says that they see no problem with giving birth to bastard children. This same batch of women **FOOLISHLY** believes they can raise a male child on their own. If this is not the case then why do they continue have them? The author **KNOWS** he isn't the only person in America that sees a problem with this attitude and the Black Community wants to know what is wrong?!

MAMA AIN'T EQUIPPED

Okay, Okay, again for the sake of argument, **IF** the author were to expound upon feasible solutions, the environment would include hard discipline, structured regiments, household responsibilities and character building self-esteem. By the "results" of what the Black Community has put into society... correction, jail, it is evident those principles were not present, enforced or very poorly addressed. Let's face it, a Black Single Mom can't do sh**, if by the time their son reaches his teens and does not want to listen to what she has to say. If in the household of a strong consistent paternal figure, the "kid gloves" would have begun to come off before the age of six. Running to Mama to get out of doing things would stop. Mama loves her BOY but Mama cannot raise a MAN, the author does not give-a-f#@* what any Black Woman says! Okay, then why the f#@* are they still trying to do it? **PRIDE**! Black Women are unwilling to say, "I ain't equipped to raise a man," and by judging the state of today's Black Community, Black Women sure as hell cannot... by themselves! In their unwillingness to let go of their *boy*, they are stifling the growth of what

> *Truth, like surgery, may hurt, but it cures.*
> --Han Suyin

it means to be a man! Some may say, "What, and just let the boy fester in the streets?" NO. The author is saying let them become part of an organization that specializes in taking those devoid of a strong consistent paternal figure, while growing-up, and turning them into something productive to function in society as a whole. What could this mean? What the author is referring to is the military and under the age of 18, military boarding schools. Sorry to say but these are the best solutions for boys sentenced to the environment Black Single Moms gave them at birth... if they truly want to correct what has gone wrong.

It is very irritating to hear Black Single Moms shun a solution, of their sons to serving in the military, when they perpetrated the problem. They do not want to see their sons in jail but they also do not want structured entities installing the required discipline to prevent it. **W-T-F!** It is the best opportunity for their boys (who did not have a strong consistent paternal figure in their lives growing-up) to learn what Mama **CAN'T** teach him: What it is to be a man!

When Black Single Moms decide to neglect these points, they are doing nothing but putting another f#@*?%-up Black Male into the community to, statistically, wreak havoc on our community and society as a whole; repeating the cycle of Black

The Wrong Stuff

Women asking why they cannot find a decent man who respects them. Hmmm! Just look at how he was raised, to include the environment from which he came, and it should give you all the answers you need. Men are not born, they are made and Mama cannot do it! If Mama cannot identify the appropriate man to serve as an example for a child then Mama should not have any damn kids! How much simpler does it get? Waiting around hoping, wishing, praying their sons turn into the likes of a Michael Eric Dyson, Ph.D., a Benjamin Carson, M.D. or Judge Greg Mathis is a pipe dream, without definitive structure. YES, these men endured very challenging childhoods and emerged to become extremely successful and intelligent men. However, what is over looked is that they are the extreme exception and not the majority; they are not just members of the 2% club but the ¼ of 1% club! We cannot build a strong Race based upon those percentages.

REFERENCE GROUPS

Male Children had no choice but to be here and now raised in an environment that says those actions taken by you, the Single Mom, were okay; that nothing was wrong with **your** decision. Thus assuring the child will repeat the cycle of screwing-up a family structure for the next generation. What family structure will your son be more likely to reproduce? The life he sees Mama providing or the structure of a conservative family? The answer is: The life he will remember growing-up; his "reference groups." The first reference group is what he sees at home, the immediate family: Is mommy married to daddy? The second reference group is the extended family: Is grandmommy married to granddaddy? Are the cousins from two-parent households? The third reference group is from the neighborhood: Are a majority of the families, with children, comprised of a mother married to the father or a bunch of Single Moms doing it themselves? The fourth reference group is from school and social groups: What kind of families and homes do these kids come from? The point the author is making is that every subsequent reference group, after the household, reinforces what is acceptable or not. If an overwhelming majority of what the boy sees consist of mothers not married to their son' father then that is what he will see as normal. Again, thus assuring he will do the same thing because he will have no respect for the institution of marriage and the role it plays in American society as a whole. If he EVER hopes to succeed on a large scale, he will interact with the white world extensively. If his only reference points, and groups, come from the *stereotypical* Black Community, he is going to have some challenges. If he uses (the only one he knows) the "Black Family Template," not adjusting to his current environment, and tries to apply it to a White society, he REALLY will have some problems (not challenges anymore!) this time. Solution? Just make sure he stays restricted in the Black world and he will not have any problems... yea right! For all the "suspect" Black Single Moms, thanks for f#@*\!$-up another Black Male's life. The real tragedy is that those Black Male Children who are not too bright will not even know how f#@*?%-up they really are to begin the prevention of continuing the cycle!

WHAT THE FUTURE HOLDS

Ye shall know the truth, and the truth shall make you free.

–THE HOLY BIBLE

JOHN 8:32

Chapter 9

WHAT THE FUTURE HOLDS

TAKE CONTROL!

The future of the Black Race is in the hands of the Black Woman. To the extent that she takes control of her body will be to the extent we begin to rise as a people. Yes, the Black Male is the leader of his kingdom but the Black Woman is the support behind the Black Man, allowing him to stand strong. In addition, the Black Male has to be born... by a woman. Genetics aside, if the household is [not in order] then, in all probability, as goes that Black Male Child. Every animal on earth that has the ability to prepare a nest for a newborn does so **BEFORE** the birth not scrambling around after-the-fact trying to put the family unit together! Maybe we should take a page out of the animals' book on parenting.

RUNNING GAME

The author hears the outcries from Black Women and Black Single Moms all the time about how they've been wronged! News Flash! If **you allow** yourself to fall into certain predicaments, how can you blame anyone else for your shortcomings? YOU ARE IN CONTROL! If you give away that power, you deserve what you get! Are there guys out here that are foul? Yes, absolutely, there are several of them but asking this one question underscores its significance: What the h*ll does that got to do with you?! You got two legs?! Walk away! There aren't many good ones available but if you cannot find just one in a pool of one million plus, then maybe you don't deserve to have a man. Another News Flash! You will have a greater chance of getting struck by lightning, in the middle of the desert, on a sunny day than one just dropping in your lap while sitting in your living room, eating Bon-Bons and watching Jeopardy. Sorry to break it to you but **YOU** are going to have to go out and get one… and he ain't at the club!

What the Future Holds

Okay, with the shortage of *viable* brothers out here, sistas are starting to do what men have been doing forever: "Running Game!" For those of you who do not know, let the author explain. It is when one party tries to get over on the other by pretending to be exclusive to party one, or at least extremely receptive, while making "moves" with party two, three, four and possibly more! Brace yourselves! Here comes the double-standard! When a guy does this (not saying it is right) society may not like it but lives with it. When a woman does this, she is considered trifling. Now, here is the issue. If a woman does not mind being called and considered a slut or a whore then everything is all-good. However, if she has reservations about being called and considered such names then maybe she should not engage in such practices. That's pretty simple... right? Women, no matter how much you wish and pray, you are not going to change society's thinking! The story below is of a female who was doing just what we were discussing, "Running Game." Not mailed in, the author is telling this one second hand.

Not using this guy's real name, we will call him Todd. He told the author about an experience about a woman he says he is not seeing but how he explained it did not quite sound right but anyway, he titled the story, "RUNNING GAME ON [blank]S!"

> She ain't slick. I knew she was running game, I've heard her running game! I over heard her with one of her girlfriends specifically say, "…if just the hint of getting the p**** is present, I can get them off some money…." One summer afternoon a lawn care representative came by her house looking to get paid for services he rendered a week ago. I immediately knew she was deceptive in getting that lawn care rep to fertilize her lawn because I knew this company to be a pay-per-treatment service so his showing up wasn't a good sign; Running Game. They made some kind of arrangement and it didn't seem like it was for money.
>
> I've witnessed her deceptive practices on three separate occasions over the phone. One time, in particular, she wanted everyone, in a particular room we were all in, to be quiet so that the guy on the other end couldn't tell who was in the room when she was speaking to him. During other instances, trying to "play" me, she has left the room to talk to [blank]s while I was there to see her!

What the Future Holds

On one of the three previous occasions, I felt sorry for one of the guys because he was really being played! I wonder if she is playing me about him, just as I KNOW she is playing him about me? Playing him while she gets money and favors out of him is her business. She can front all she wants but I know he's f#@*?% her and I've just watched her make a fool out-of-herself telling me otherwise of how she doesn't f#@* married men. Ironically, during one conversation we had, she told me of the type of person she despises; one who doesn't tell the truth! She's an example of one of those Black Single Mothers you (the author) were telling me about; doing *whatever* it takes to pay those bills.

Women. Whatever it takes? Whatever you need to do to make ends meet is your business but please understand, that precedent, as it pertains to men, will come to your son's attention eventually. Women. Is that what you want, do you even care or does it even matter? In addition, you can forget about finding a male companion worth two cents acting in this manner as a way of life.

GUYS' PERCEPTION

Women. Is it important how a man perceives you? Does it matter if it is a boyfriend, fiancée or husband? You may say, of course it matters or maybe some of you could care less! Why does, or doesn't, it matter? It comes down to the value you put on varying levels of a relationship. Does that sound about accurate? Okay, if this is the case, regardless of whether or not you care about the particular level of your male companion, a serious relationship **starts** out as boyfriend & girlfriend. Yea, yea, I know there are some cultures where the man and women meet for the first time the day of the marriage ceremony but there will not be to many of them reading this book either. The point the author is making is that in our culture, we build-up to marriage via dating. Women, your habitual inclinations

> *...when you have eliminated the impossible, whatever remains, however improbable, must be the truth.*
> --Sir Arthur Conan Doyle

don't just disintegrate when you exchange "I do's." All of your, what you may not think of as, quirky, questionable tendencies while dating will be ingrained into your male companion's mind during this period. What perception of yourself do you want to leave in his mind moving forward? Remember that perception does not start at marriage... it starts now.

Women, let the author tell you of a cruel joke nature plays on the sexes. The cruelty lies in nature giving us an extremely strong desire for a very particular thing but simultaneously knowing full well that it HARD-WIRED each sex for a reaction totally different from what the opposite sex wants! *The want* without *the ability* to reach fruition! What could that be?

A man sees a woman as a snapshot; a still picture in time. Broaden a little, he is going to remember the woman (forever) as she was over the initial period of their dating. The **present** not the future.

A woman sees a man as a movie; what is it that she can do to make the story a happy ending! She doesn't care what's going on now, she sees grandkids! The **future** not the present.

Stated slightly different earlier, a man is going to remember you as you are TODAY.

The fact is, he as your *boyfriend*, you have no obligation to tell him anything: what you do, with whom, at your "business meetings" or where you go. Even if going off to where ever for several questionable hours. Yes, you are an *unmarried* woman, but just understand that you are setting a precedent you may not be able to shake later. It may not look foul to you and you may think that the onus is on him to ask but actually, it is on you to divulge information. If you tell him all your business or omit everything, it speaks volumes. The question comes down to what do **you** want *your actions* to say. If you were to ask the author what he thinks they (actions pertaining to "suspect" behavior) were saying, words associated to women of really low quality come to mind but that is only the opinion of the author. Point here is that you do not know how the relationship will progress so **it is** important how he perceives you now.

The author had a mentor that told him something pertaining to politics decades ago that has some relevance to this situation now. He would always say, "You don't vote or act the way you are today but where you see yourself tomorrow." This simply translates into: If you enter relationships as if you are going to marry this person in the future then how should you act today? Based on

What the Future Holds

everything previously mentioned, the chances are that it will not be your *acting* like a slut.

The passage below is from a correspondence to a woman, referencing a change in perception.

> One afternoon, we had a discussion over the phone about your curiosities of private clubs that engage in extremely promiscuous behavior, where each level (floor) had an increasing level of intensity. Things ranging from the very mild voyeurism, upwards to multiple partner interactions and beyond. The next day, you called me to make sure that I didn't think poorly of you because of your curiosity and put you in the "questionable" category, which, of course, was too late anyway. That was then, when you cared about what I thought. Now you probably don't give-a-f#@* what I think: you know we are not long-term; that you might as well do what you want to do and; since you believe that I already think poorly of you anyway, you've got nothing to lose. Based on how this usually progresses, I'm sure you will find yourself back in one of those private clubs (which I'm sure you have already) by yourself or with your girls, exploring your curiosities.
>
> *Jeff --*

HEY! YOU'VE GOT OPTIONS!

Women, suppose you say, "I want a higher quality of guy other than the four types mentioned in the section, 'Scrapping the Bottom,' in Chapter Two." You *may* have at least three options:

One, you could wait until your son is 18 and moved cross country (highly unlikely if your boy is a little soft; needs his Mama to take him every where because he is a Mama's boy);

> *A lie told often enough becomes the truth.*
> --Vladimir Lenin (1870 - 1924)

Two, make-up lies that are appealing to an intellectual (something you will need to be good at, to pull it off) e.g. "My husband died in an accident before my son was a year old." As opposed to, "The boy's father and I never married because we just didn't get along, he had a girlfriend and some other kids somewhere but I wanted a son anyway. Over 21, I was grown and I didn't need no man to take care of my baby for me." (all which **is considered ghetto trifling** in polite society)

The third option – You can *give* him a reason to "pay" a PREMIUM. This means that every aspect, outside your having a son, **HAD-BETTER-BE** immaculate to counterbalance, and tremendously over shadow, what will be seen as a deal breaker. You must be on point with everything: **mentally** (impressive education, emotionally stable, understands what a man wants, can engage in diverse conversation); **physically** (an attractive Head Shot, a fit body, disease free health); **financially** (a respectable and promising career and a boat load of comforts that comes with an above average income) and; **socially** (professionally well connected, accomplished friends, prestigious social groups & community involvement). What this tells a man is that she is doing okay without him so she is not after what he has to bring him down. In addition, if she is that thorough, it will be reflective in her son and that will further attract a higher caliber of man. All this is relative, of course, to what is most appealing to the man. No man is expecting every PREMIUM but you need to have more in your favor than the average woman, without kids, to get him to focus his attention on you and not your "competition."

When several of the reasons for a man to pay a PREMIUM are missing, it seriously dilutes this approach altogether. The man is no longer interested in "the pursuit of," which totally negates what PREMIUMS are all about. This is all to say that the woman must now focus on INCENTIVES.

INCENTIVES v. PREMIUMS

PREMIUMS - As mentioned earlier, these are the qualities a woman displays, to distract the guy from seeing **any** problem with her having a kid. In order to keep the focus totally on her, her "package" has to be so thorough that **he** will do things to pursue her as opposed to her trying to get him. PREMIUMS will call upon everything in her, to transform her life for the better! Translation: WORK! Black Women this ambitious and driven do not have children under 30 anyway, especially out of wedlock if they ever have plans to marry a *viable* man. They are smart enough to know the negative impact it will have on their chances of attracting that quality man. The premise is simple: A man will "pay" a PREMIUM for quality but must be given INCENTIVES to buy "damage goods."

INCENTIVES - When your ability to fetch a PREMIUM is not even worth mentioning then you really are "Damaged Goods" and you cannot *expect* top dollar (a quality man). In fact, you **must** offer INCENTIVES to even get the

"Crap" to want to buy (marry) you. INCENTIVES are the *benefits* a Black Woman has to give in order to persuade even a dumb-ass-[n*****] to stick around, all in an effort to neutralize issues pertaining to a kid(s). Instead of improving on purposeful matters (mind, health, finance, social connections, etc.) enticing him to pursue her, she is now in pursuit of him by providing everything she can for him to stay: sex, shelter, she cooks, cleans, buys his clothes, provides transportation and in most cases, he doesn't even need to work. All the guy has to do is just be around. Her objective is to make everything so care free that, in the guy's mind, he would be crazy to leave. If a man has to go through all the normal routines of being a provider **AND** then have to put up with some other man's bastard son, he has got to be stupid as f#@*;   hence the bottom of the socio-economic scale! INCENTIVES are the equalizer to keep him from looking *that* stupid or at least to minimize it!

The truth is, the higher you go up the intellectual ladder, the less receptive a man, who has a future (outside of entertainment), is going to be towards a bastard child. With the passing of every stage (there are five) of child development, your chances of getting and keeping (marriage) a quality man diminishes considerably. If you haven't turned the trick by stage 4 (before 12 years old) forget it! To attract the "A" Buyer (the top 5% of the Black Male population) you must provide INCENTIVES. The "A" Buyer will rarely buy anything on discount whether it is a good deal or not (clothing, hotels, restaurants, companionship, etc.) anyway. If you are not going to put forth the work to entice a quality man **to pursue you**, just stick with giving INCENTIVES to the dumb-ass-[n******], you will inevitably meet going to places they frequent.

EPILOGUE

Now that you have finished the book, you may have noticed that there are no summations at the end of the chapters. Why? Well, it should be clear as to what my opinions are, up until this point, so it is time for you to give your summation! As I eluded to in the Preface, this book is not finished. The chapter endings are the points from which the debate will begin, the beginning of how to reverse the continuing cycle of illegitimate births.

We can now begin the journey of an open dialogue and it leading to eventual change. You may begin either by going to MamasFault.com, or to several of the other social networking sites under the name "Mamas Fault," to submit your comments. It will be from there where you may communicate with other concerned voices about the same subject matter.

Is it too late to change the lives of adults born out of such circumstances, in order to prevent the destruction of the next generation? In all probability, yep! But ultimately that's up to them not me. However, NOW is the time to positively influence the minds of the very young into internalizing the notion that a nuclear family structure proceeds the birth of a child, when given a choice. The author has some solutions but what are yours? The *revised* edition of "It's Mama's Fault!" is waiting for your input! We'll see you online!

Lex Drás

RECOMMENDED READING

Family Secrets: What You Don't Know Can Hurt You by John Bradshaw. 1995. ISBN 9780553095913

Your Man & His Mother by Annette Annechild. 1992. ISBN 9780681414662

Mothers, Sons, and Lovers : How a Man's Relationship with His Mother Affects the Rest of His Life by Michael Gurian. 1994. ISBN 9780877739456

Ten Stupid Things Women Do To Mess Up Their Lives by Laura Schlessinger. 1995. ISBN 9780060976491

Come On, People: On the Path from Victims to Victors by Bill Cosby. 2007. ISBN 9781595550927

Is Bill Cosby Right? Or Has the Black Middle Class Lost Its Mind? by Michael Eric Dyson. 2005. ISBN 9780465017195

Why I Love Black Women by Michael Eric Dyson. 2003. ISBN 9780465017683

Gifted Hands: The Ben Carson Story by Ben Carson. 1996. ISBN 978031021469

Inner City Miracle by Greg Mathis. 2002. ISBN 9780345446428

Whatever Happened to Daddy's Little Girl?: The Impact of Fatherlessness on Black Women by Jonetta Rose Barras. 2000. ISBN 9780345422460

Secrets about Men Every Woman Should Know by Barbara DiAngeles. 1990. ISBN 9780385299619

A Woman's Worth by Marianne Williamson. 1993. ISBN 978067942218

INDEX

D

E

high quality, xx, 76

Historically Black Colleges & Universities, 57

history, 108, 114, 138

hoe, xxv, 87, 103, 112, 115

home, 48, 70, 72, 73, 77, 87, 94, 150

hookers, 134

house, 65, 78, 81, 97, 104, 132, 137, 158

household, 54, 71, 74, 86, 133, 144, 146, 150, 155

husband, 160, 164

hypocritical, xxx, 74

I

idea, xxv, 38, 73

identify, xxv, xxvii, 149

illegitimate, xix, xx, xxiii, xxvi, 75, clxix

impact, xx, 73, 129, 166

impossible, 39

INCENTIVE, 166, 168

income, 59, 65, 75, 131, 165

inevitably, 34, 128, 143, 168

information, 42, 162

initial, xxiv, 34, 42, 61, 114, 126, 161

integrity, 133

intellect, xxvii, 103

intellectual, 109, 131, 164, 167

intelligent, xx, xxiii, 41, 101, 113, 116, 149

interactions, xxvii, 114, 163

intercourse, 50

Internet, 128

irrevocable, xxvii, 77, 144

Ivy League, 78

J

Jackson, Samuel L.. *See* Movies: Black Snake Moan

jail, 147

Jeopardy, 156

job, 55, 75, 128

judgement, xxvii, 41, 43

K

kid, 74, 147, 167

kids, 42, 48, 55, 58, 82, 85, 105, 149, 150, 165

killing, xxiii, xxvi, 50

kiss, 34, 113

knowledge, 58, 114

L

language, 34, 121, 122

leadership, xxviii

learn, 71, 106, 114, 148

legal, x

Liberal, 75

life, xxvi, 33, 36, 37, 54, 56, 71, 73, 76, 81, 89, 105, 124, 133, 150, 159, 166

live, xx, 37, 133, 135

Logic, xxvii, 60

Loneliness, xxvi

Q

R

S

U

V

W

Is it Mama's Fault?

Give your input

AND

Join the conversation

at:

MamasFAULT.com

ORDER FORM

Use this convenient order form to obtain additional copies of

"It's Mama's Fault!"
Poor Decisions Psychologically Damaging the Male Child

Please Print:

Name - Mr.( ) Ms. ( ) _____

Address - _____

City_____ State - _____

Zip - _____

Phone – (   ) _____

_____ Copies of this book @ $ _17.95_ each $ _____

S&H @ $ _4.70_ / book $ _____

GA residents add _6_ % tax $ _____

Total amount enclosed $ _____

Make checks payable to Group Publishing House, LLC
P. O. Box 723921, Atlanta, Georgia 31139

For a complete schedule regarding bulk purchase discounts
and this book in other formats, please click the
"Download" Button at:
www.MamasFault.com

Is it Mama's Fault?

Give your input

AND

Join the conversation

at:

MamasFAULT.com

ORDER FORM

Use this convenient order form to obtain additional copies of

"It's Mama's Fault!"
Poor Decisions Psychologically Damaging the Male Child

Please Print:

Name - Mr.( ) Ms. ( ) _____

Address - _____

City_____ State - _____

Zip - _____

Phone – (   ) _____

_____ Copies of this book @ $ _17.95_ each $ _____

S&H @ $ _4.70_ / book $ _____

GA residents add _6_ % tax $ _____

Total amount enclosed $ _____

Make checks payable to Group Publishing House, LLC
P. O. Box 723921, Atlanta, Georgia 31139

For a complete schedule regarding bulk purchase discounts
and this book in other formats, please click the
"Download" Button at:
www.MamasFault.com

CPSIA information can be obtained at www.ICGtesting.com
Printed in the USA
BVOW03s0953140514

353506BV00014B/289/P